THE TWO TOWERS

A JOURNEY SUPPLEMENT FOR
THE LORD OF THE RINGS STRATEGY BATTLE GAME

*"How shall any tower withstand
such numbers and such reckless hate?"*

The Two Towers

CONTENTS

Inspired by the works of
John R. R. Tolkien.

By
Graham McNeill, Adam Troke,
Mark Jones, Dominic Murray & Adrian Wood

Additional Material
Mat Ward, Neil Hodgson & Chad Mierzwa

Graphic Design
Markus Trenkner

Conceptual Design
Rick Priestley & Alessio Cavatore

Miniatures Design
Alan Perry, Michael Perry

Production
Michelle Barson, Chris Eggar,
Marc Elliott, Dylan Owen,
Mark Owen, Adam Shaw
& Ian Strickland

'Eavy Metal
Fil Dunn, Pete Foley, Neil Green,
Neil Langdown, Darren Latham, Keith Robertson,
Kirsten Williams & Anya Wettergren

Special Thanks To...
Peter Jackson, Richard Taylor & everybody at Weta. John Mayo, David Imhoff & Trevor Wilson at New Line Cinema. Laurie Battle, Fredrica Drotos & Joe Mandragona at Tolkien Enterprises. Nelson, Andy Jones & The Ringwraiths

PRODUCED BY GAMES WORKSHOP

Games Workshop The Lord of The Rings website
http://uk.games-workshop.com/thelordoftherings/

Games Workshop website
www.games-workshop.com

The Lord of The Rings website:
www.lordoftherings.net

UK
Games Workshop,
Willow Rd,
Lenton,
Nottingham, NG7 2WS

US
Games Workshop,
6711 Baymeadow Drive,
Glen Burnie,
Maryland 21060-6401

Australia
Games Workshop,
23 Liverpool Street,
Ingleburn
NSW 2565

Canada
2679 Bristol Circle
Unit 3,
Oakville,
Ontario L6H 6Z8

Northern Europe
Games Workshop,
Willow Rd,Lenton,
Nottingham, NG7 2WS
UK

NEW LINE CINEMA
A Time Warner Company

Tolkien Enterprises

AOL keyword:
Lord of the Rings

INTRODUCTION

Welcome to The Two Towers, the second of a new range of The Lord of The Rings Strategy Battle Game supplements. This supplement is an ideal follow-on to The Fellowship of The Ring or the main rules manual, and you will need a copy of the rules to make full use of the gaming material presented here. It's not essential to have played The Fellowship of The Ring before embarking on The Two Towers, but you'll enjoy the campaign a lot more if you've already travelled with Frodo from Bag End to Amon Hen!

After the breaking of the Fellowship, Frodo and Sam must travel a different path from their companions in their quest to destroy the Ring. In The Two Towers we've split the campaign into three sections; the adventures of Aragorn, Legolas and Gimli, Frodo's journey to Mordor and finally the great battle at Helm's Deep.

The main pages of this supplement cover three subjects:

 SCENARIOS

 PAINTING

 TERRAIN

The scenarios link together into a campaign that allows you to play through the key events of the book and the film. As the Good player, you take control of the Heroes of the Free Peoples – Hobbits, Men, Dwarves and Elves. As the Evil player, you have the chance to do what Sauron's minions could not, slay Frodo and enslave all of Middle-earth to your will. Use Dunlending Warriors to destroy the folk of Rohan, evil servants of the Witch-king to hunt Frodo, and Uruk-hai to storm the bastion of Helm's Deep.

The supplement will also help you collect and paint all the models you need. Detailed guides cover the techniques you'll need to get your models painted and looking great.

You'll also be shown how to build the terrain you need to play the scenarios. You don't have to build these, as you'll be shown a number of others ways to represent terrain. Having said that, it's worth having a go, as dramatic terrain really sets the scene for the battles of The Two Towers.

When you reach the end of this supplement, you'll have decided the fate of the Heroes of the Fellowship and built a substantial collection of models and terrain that you can use to play all manner of other battles.

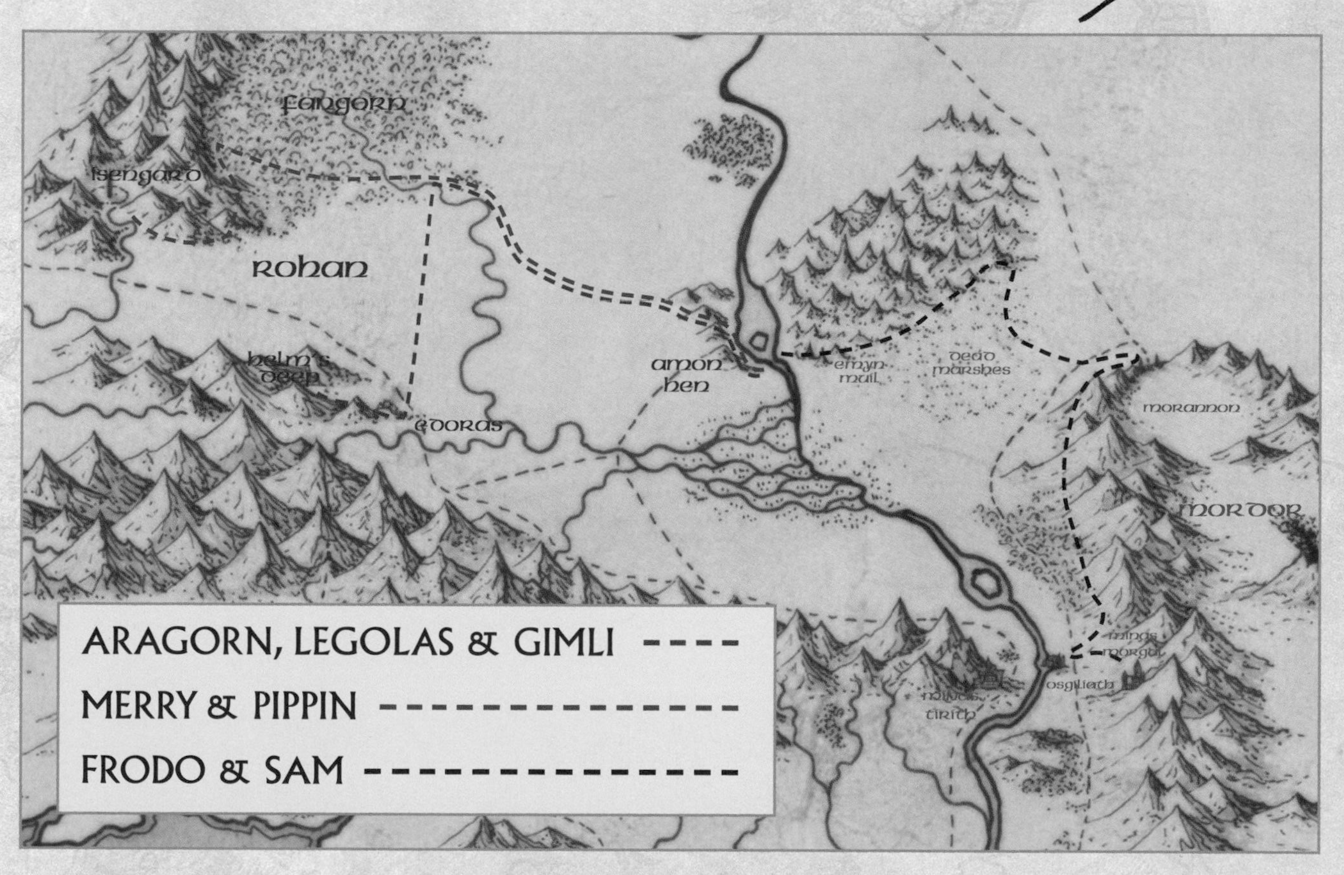

The routes of the Fellowship

HOW TO USE THIS SUPPLEMENT

The pages of this supplement are divided into three types: Scenarios, Painting and Terrain. Each page type is explained here.

SCENARIOS

Each scenario depicts a particular scene from The Two Towers film or book. Played in order, they follow through the entire story

At the back of this supplement you will find a more advanced way to link the scenarios, to form a continuing adventure. There is also a summary of the profiles for all the model warriors and creatures you will need to play.

The dice icon denotes a Scenario page.

The story – setting the scene for this encounter.

'Objectives' describes what each side must do to win.

The photograph shows the game in progress, using the scenery described on the Terrain pages, and models painted as shown in the Painting pages.

'Layout' explains how to set up the terrain – this is also shown on the board map.

'Participants' lists the models required on each side to fight this scenario.

'Starting Positions' details where to deploy your models (again this may be illustrated on the map).

The scenarios all have 'Special Rules' which apply only for that particular battle.

'Points Match' explains how to use the scenario with different models to those listed.

EQUIPMENT

You will see in The Lord of The Rings rules manual that many characters have various options for the equipment they carry, or mounts they ride. For the scenarios in this supplement, players should choose whichever options best match the relevant scene in the film or book. For example, Gandalf the White is used in The Two Towers as opposed to Gandalf the Grey.

PAINTING

As the story progresses, these pages provide instructions and tips for painting the miniatures required in the scenarios.

On Painting and Terrain pages, the different paints are symbolised by coloured circles:

●● means use one colour followed by the next.

◐ means to mix the colours.

Painting pages are marked by this icon.

Simple techniques and painting tips will help you get great results.

A photograph of the finished model shows what to aim for.

Step-by-step guides show how we have painted the models shown.

Colour guides show the specific Citadel Colour paints used on the models.

TERRAIN

The Terrain pages show how to make model scenery to represent Middle-earth. Many of the terrain pieces are multi-purpose and can be used for many different battles.

A page showing all the tools and materials you will need to complete the terrain projects can be found at the back of the book.

'Materials' lists all the things you will need to make this piece.

Particular techniques are highlighted.

A modelling knife shows these are Terrain pages.

Each terrain project has step-by-step photographs, explaining clearly what to do.

May of these are key techniques that can be applied to other terrain examples in this book as well. This is a good way to ensure your terrain collection all matches.

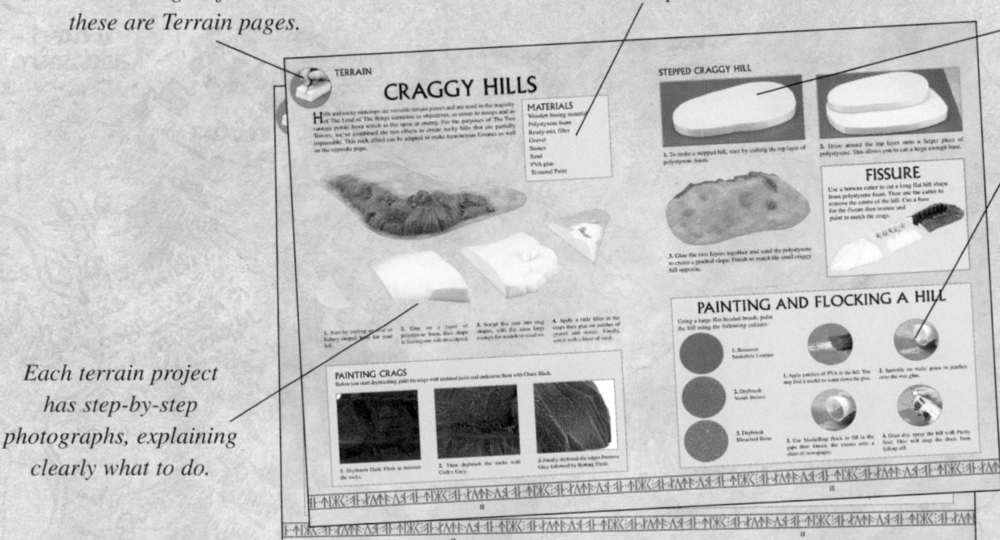

THE TREASON OF ISENGARD

The War of the Ring has begun and the forces of the traitor Saruman march south out of the dungeons of Isengard. Armies of bestial Uruk-hai and ferocious Dunlending Warriors march upon Rohan, land of King Théoden, intent on nothing less than its utter destruction. Aragorn, Legolas and Gimli set off in pursuit of the Uruk-hai Scouts who have taken Merry and Pippin prisoner as the invasion begins. King Théoden sits withered and decrepit on his throne, held enfeebled by Saruman's power and Rohan is ready to fall. But Rohan is not without heroes, and its Captains rally their warriors to fight the invading armies and save their homeland from destruction.

Merry and Pippin's fate lies not in Isengard, but in the depths of Fangorn Forest where they encounter creatures as strange as any they have met before. The company of Aragorn travels deep into Rohan as Saruman's invasion continues, heading inexorably towards a fateful battle at the great fortress of Helm's Deep…

THE FELLOWSHIP OF THE RING TERRAIN

From the tower of Orthanc to the stronghold of Helm's Deep, The Two Towers features vast landscapes and impregnable fortresses. In this book we show how to recreate some of the key terrain that features in this part of the story for use in your games.

If you've already played through The Fellowship of The Ring supplement you will be familiar with the idea of playing scenarios using a board full of terrain. Much of that scenery can also be used in The Two Towers.

URUK-HAI SCOUTS

The Uruk-hai Scouts take Merry and Pippin captive at Saruman's command. These lightly armoured hunters are strong and skilful warriors who fight in all scenarios set in Rohan except Warg Attack (scenario 6), The Last March of the Ents (scenario 8) and The Battle For Helm's Deep (scenarios 13-17).

URUK-HAI SCOUTS

- **Hair:** Chaos Black, Codex Grey
- **Leather:** Scorched Brown, Scorched Brown/Bleached Bone
- **Skin:** Dark Flesh, Brown Ink, Dark Flesh/Bleached Bone

DRYBRUSHING

For this technique, you'll need to use a Drybrush, and some fairly thick paint. Work the colour into the brush and then wipe any excess back onto the palette. Begin by stroking the brush gently over the surface that you wish to highlight. The brush should deposit a fine, even dusting of colour over the raised areas of the model.

URUK-HAI ARMOUR

Start by drybrushing all armour with Tin Bitz.

To finish, drybrush with Chainmail.

VRASKÛ

Vraskû commands the Scout Uruk-hai of Isengard. He is both cunning and resourceful, and his twin-shot crossbow is the terror of his enemies.

Models such as this benefit from a little more time painting their extra details.

FERAL URUK-HAI

Consumed with blood lust, feral Uruk-hai warriors wear little armour and carry two hand weapons. They share the same palette as the Uruk-hai Scouts.

ORCS

Orcs fight both for the Wizard Saruman and the Dark Lord Sauron. They use sheer weight of numbers to overwhelm their opponents, appearing in the Wrath of Rohan (scenario 4), Alone in Fangorn (scenario 5), The Last March of the Ents (scenario 8), Osgiliath (scenario 12) and The Siege of Helm's Deep (scenario 17).

ORCS

- **Armour:** Tin Bitz, Chainmail
- **Hair:** Graveyard Earth
- **Leather:** Scorched Brown, Dark Flesh
- **Skin:** Catachan Green or Camo Green or Codex Grey

LAYERING

Layering is a highlighting technique achieved by painting successively lighter graduations of colour on a model. Painting layers over a black undercoat provides highlights that are simple to achieve and look effective. With practice you'll be able to add more layers of colour, thereby creating a more subtle appearance.

ORC TUNIC

Basecoat with a mix of Chaos Black and Codex Grey.

Layer a highlight of Codex Grey onto the model.

Apply a final highlight mix of Codex Grey and Bleached Bone.

GRISHNÁKH

The cunning Grishnákh is painted the same as other Orcs but is distinguished by his red skin colour.

GRISHNÁKH

- **Bones:** Bubonic Brown, Bleached Bone
- **Skin:** Dark Flesh, Vermin Brown

BASING

The easiest way to add textured material to a base is to paint it with PVA glue and then dip it into a tray of modelling sand. Once the sand is dry, paint it with the following colours:

- Scorched Brown
- Bestial Brown
- Bleached Bone

Finally, paint the edge of the base Bestial Brown. To complete the base, dab on patches of PVA glue and then sprinkle it with static grass.

ARAGORN

Aragorn is a Ranger and the future King of Men – one of the greatest warriors of the age. He is one of the central characters in The Two Towers and appears in Let's Hunt Some Orc (scenario 1), Warg Attack (scenario 6) and The Battle For Helm's Deep (scenarios 13-17).

ARAGORN

Boots: Scorched Brown, Scorched Brown/ Bleached Bone

Skin: Dark Flesh, Dwarf Flesh, Chestnut Ink, Dwarf Flesh

Hair: Scorched Brown, Bestial Brown

Sleeves: Shadow Grey, Fortress Grey

Sword: Boltgun Metal, Chainmail, Mithril Silver

INK WASHES

An ink wash is a fast way of shading a colour. Water is added to an ink or paint to thin it down slightly, and this is then applied over a light base colour. The ink will run into the crevices and folds of a model providing natural looking shading.

CLOTH

Basecoat the cloth with Scorched Brown.

Apply a Brown Ink wash and leave to dry thoroughly.

Layer on an equal parts mix of Scorched Brown and Bleached Bone.

Add more Bleached Bone to the mix and apply final highlights.

MERRY

A brave Hobbit from the Shire, Merry is as cheerful as his name suggests. It is thanks to this loyal and brave Hobbit that Treebeard and the Ents join the fight against Isengard.

MERRY

Coat: Dark Angels Green, Goblin Green

Hair: Snakebite Leather, Desert Yellow, Bleached Bone

Skin: Dwarf Flesh, Elf Flesh

Sword: Boltgun Metal, Chainmail

Trousers: Scorched Brown, Bleached Bone

Waistcoat: Vomit Brown, Bubonic Brown

PIPPIN

Pippin is Merry's closest friend, and maintains the deception that they are the Hobbits sought by the Uruk-hai. When the chance arrives, he and Merry flee to the dubious safety of Fangorn.

PIPPIN

Coat: Regal Blue, Ultramarines Blue

Hair: Bestial Brown, Vomit Brown

Leather: Scorched Brown, Bestial Brown

Scarf: Codex Grey, Fortress Grey

Shirt: Fortress Grey, Skull White

Skin: Dwarf Flesh, Elf Flesh

Sword: Boltgun Metal, Chainmail

Trousers: Scorched Brown, Bestial Brown

LEGOLAS

Legolas is an Elf who hails from Mirkwood. A deadly archer, he fights alongside Aragorn and Gimli in Let's Hunt Some Orc (scenario 1), Warg Attack (scenario 6) and The Battle For Helm's Deep (scenarios 13-17).

PALETTE

Bow: Scorched Brown, Dark Flesh, Bestial Brown

Daggers: Boltgun Metal, Chainmail, Mithril Silver

Gold trim: Shining Gold, Chestnut Ink, Burnished Gold

Hair: Vomit Brown, Desert Yellow, Bleached Bone

Leather: Scorched Brown, Scorched Brown/Bleached Bone

Leggings: Shadow Grey, Fortress Grey

Quiver: Dark Flesh, Bestial Brown

Skin: Tanned Flesh, Dwarf Flesh, Dwarf Flesh/Elf Flesh

TUNIC

Paint the tunic Dark Angels Green.

Then apply a layer of Snot Green.

Highlight with Goblin Green.

GIMLI

Gimli is a Dwarf warrior from Erebor. He is powerful in hand-to-hand combat and together with Aragorn and Legolas appears in Let's Hunt Some Orc (scenario 1), Warg Attack (scenario 6) and The Battle For Helm's Deep (scenarios 13-17).

PALETTE

Beard: Dark Flesh, Dark Flesh/Bleached Bone

Chainmail & axe blades: Boltgun Metal, Chainmail, Mithril Silver

Gold trim: Brazen Brass, Shining Gold

Axe haft: Dark Flesh, Bestial Brown

Leather: Scorched Brown, Bestial Brown, Bleached Bone.

Skin: Tanned Flesh, Dwarf Flesh, Chestnut Ink, Elf Flesh

Tunic: Scorched Brown/Scab Red, Red Gore

HELMET

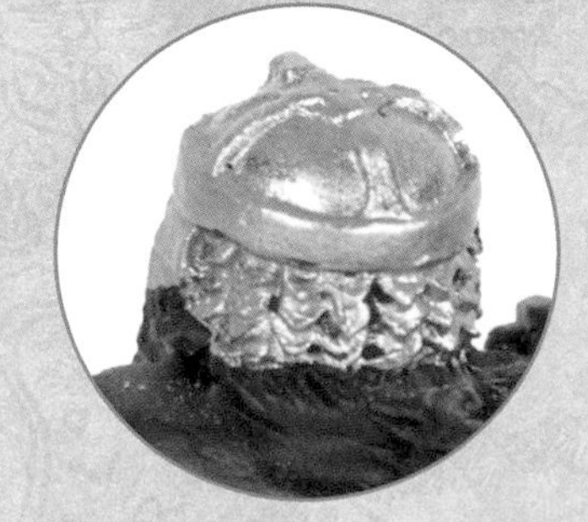

Paint a base colour of Chainmail.

Apply a Black Ink wash.

Paint the details with Shining Gold.

CRAGGY HILLS

Hills and rocky outcrops are versatile terrain pieces and are used in the majority of The Lord of The Rings scenarios: as objectives, as cover to troops and as vantage points from which to fire upon an enemy. For the purposes of The Two Towers, we've combined the two effects to create rocky hills that are partially impassable. This rock effect can be adapted to make treacherous fissures as well on the opposite page.

MATERIALS

Wooden basing material
Polystyrene foam
Ready-mix filler
Gravel
Stones
Sand
PVA glue
Textured paint

1. Start by cutting an oval or kidney-shaped base for your hill.

2. Glue on a layer of polystyrene foam, then shape it, leaving one side unsculpted.

3. Sculpt this area into crag shapes, with flat areas large enough for models to stand on.

4. Apply a little filler to the crags then glue on patches of gravel and stones. Finally, cover with a layer of sand.

PAINTING CRAGS

Before you start drybrushing, paint the crags with textured paint and undercoat them with Chaos Black.

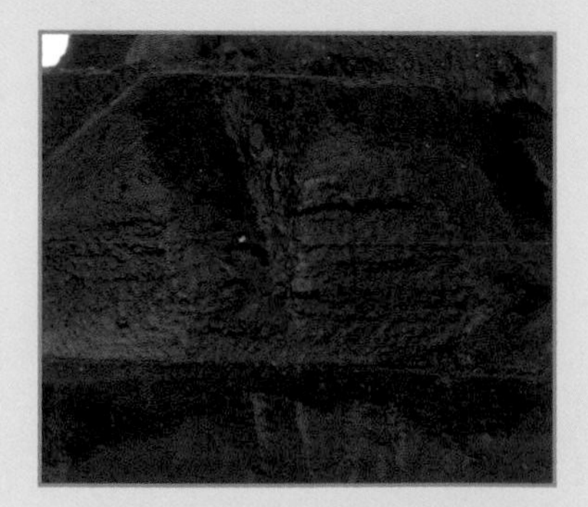

1. Drybrush Dark Flesh in between the rocks.

2. Then drybrush the rocks with Codex Grey.

3. Finally drybrush the edges Fortress Grey followed by Rotting Flesh.

STEPPED CRAGGY HILL

1. To make a stepped hill, start by cutting the top layer of polystyrene foam.

2. Draw around the top layer onto a larger piece of polystyrene. This allows you to cut a large enough base.

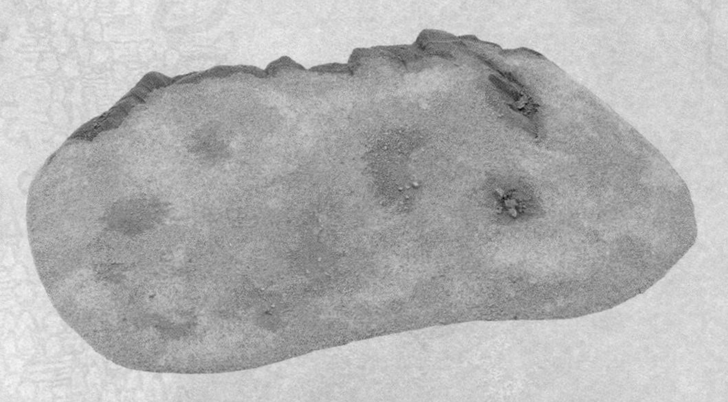

3. Glue the two layers together and sand the polystyrene to create a gradual slope. Finish to match the small craggy hill opposite.

FISSURE

Use a hot-wire cutter to cut a long flat hill shape from polystyrene foam. Then use the cutter to remove the centre of the hill. Cut a base for the fissure then texture and paint to match the crags.

PAINTING AND FLOCKING A HILL

Using a large flat-headed brush, paint the hill using the following colours:

1. Basecoat
Snakebite Leather

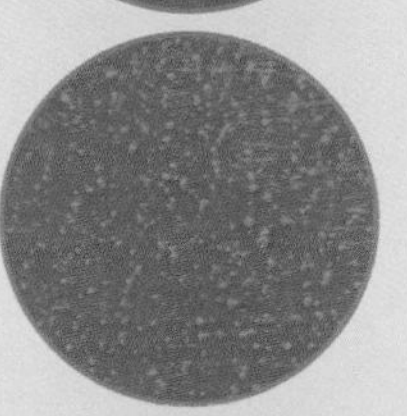

2. Drybrush
Vomit Brown

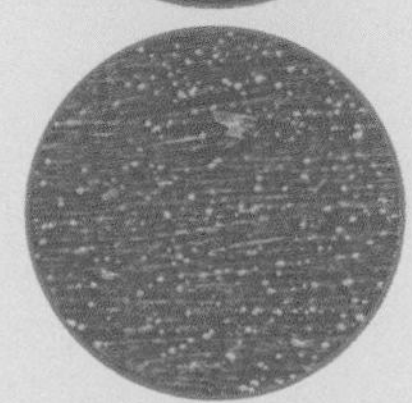

3. Drybrush
Bleached Bone

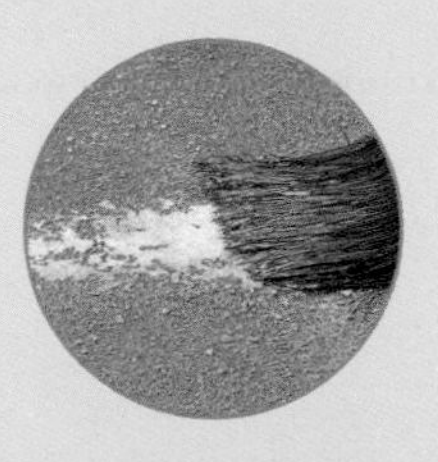

1. Apply patches of PVA to the hill. You may find it useful to water down the glue.

2. Sprinkle on static grass in patches onto the wet glue.

3. Use modelling flock to fill in the gaps then knock the excess onto a sheet of newspaper.

4. Once dry, spray the hill with Purity Seal. This will stop the flock from falling off.

SCENARIO 1

LET'S HUNT SOME ORC

The Fellowship is broken. After the attack of the Uruk-hai at Amon Hen, Boromir lies slain, Sam and Frodo have chosen their own path to Mordor and Merry and Pippin have been captured by Saruman's Uruk-hai. Aragorn, Legolas and Gimli resolve that they shall not fail their friends and set out to rescue the Hobbits from the clutches of the Uruk-hai. The Uruk-hai have a head start on Aragorn and his companions, and have despatched a force of warriors to ambush any that dare pursue. Can Aragorn's company break through to save Merry and Pippin?

PARTICIPANTS

GOOD

Aragorn/Strider with Andúril and Elven cloak
Legolas with Elven cloak
Gimli with Elven cloak

EVIL

8 Uruk-hai Scouts
4 Uruk-hai Scouts with sword and shield
3 Uruk-hai Scouts with Orc bow

"We must follow the Orcs, if there is hope that any of our Company are living prisoners."

Gimli, The Two Towers.

LAYOUT

The scenario is played on a board 24"/56cm by 24"/56cm. This encounter takes place the rocky pathways north and west of Amon Hen. As such, the ground is strewn with the occasional rocky outcrop and two rocky hills (see map).

STARTING POSITIONS

The Good player places his models touching the eastern board edge, within 3"/8cm of the middle of the board edge. The Evil player then divides his force into three roughly equal groups, deploying one group touching each of the western, southern and northern board edges. No model may be deployed within 12"/28cm of an enemy model.

POINTS MATCH

Good (450 points)

Must be composed entirely of Heroes and nominate one Hero to take the place of Aragorn. No Good models may ride steeds of any kind.

Evil (175 points)

No more than a third of the Evil models may be armed with bows or crossbows and none may ride steeds of any kind.

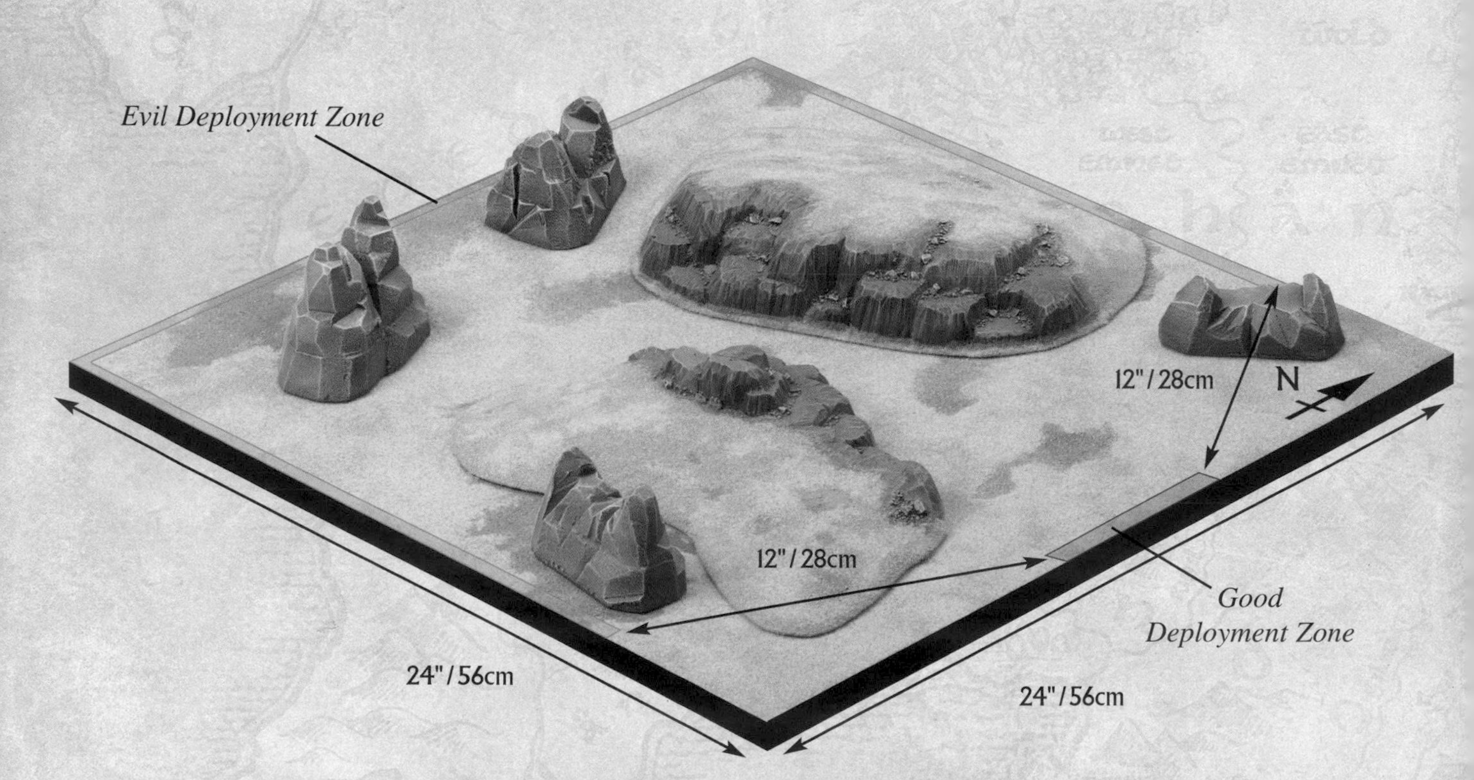

OBJECTIVES

Time is of the essence, and if Aragorn and his company cannot break through the Uruk-hai quickly, then Merry and Pippin may be lost forever. The Good player wins if Aragorn and at least one other Good model escapes from the western board edge by the end of turn seven. The Evil player wins if he manages to prevent this.

SPECIAL RULES

Forth the Three Hunters: Though pursuing the Orcs with great vigour, the three Good Heroes are weary after the battle atop Amon Hen. To represent this, Aragorn, Legolas and Gimli start the game with their Might, Will and Fate points reduced to 1 (though Aragorn's Mighty Hero rule still applies as normal).

ROHAN

The warriors of Rohan dwell in the huge grasslands of the Riddermark. They are expert horsemen and central to The Battles for the Fords of Isen (scenario 2 and 7), The Scouring of the Westfold (scenario 3), The Wrath of Rohan (scenario 4), Warg Attack (scenario 6) and The Battle For Helm's Deep (scenarios 13-17).

ROHAN

Axe/spear hafts, bows: Dark Flesh, Tanned Flesh

Cloaks: Dark Angels Green, Snot Green

Gold trim: Shining Gold, Chestnut Ink

Hair: Desert Yellow or Bronzed Flesh

Leather: Scorched Brown, Bestial Brown

Metal: Boltgun Metal, Chainmail, Black Ink, Mithril Silver

Red cloth: Scab Red, Bronzed Flesh

Shield boss: Bleached Bone, Skull White

Shield colours: Dark Flesh or Dark Angels Green

Skin: Tanned Flesh, Dwarf Flesh

These Heroes of Rohan are painted in the same way as the warriors, with any differences detailed below.

THÉODEN

Armour: Scorched Brown, Bestial Brown

Gold trim: Burnished Gold, Mithril Silver

Hair: Desert Yellow, Bleached Bone

Skin: Dwarf Flesh/Codex Grey, Brown Ink, Dwarf Flesh/Bleached Bone

Sleeves: Red Gore, Bronzed Flesh

Horse: Fortress Grey, Skull White

THÉODRED

Armour: Catachan Green, Fortress Grey

Hair: Snakebite Leather, Bleached Bone

Horse: Scorched Brown, Scorched Brown/Bleached Bone

Gold trim: Burnished Gold, Mithril Silver

Sleeves: Red Gore, Bronzed Flesh

ÉOMER

Armour: Scab Red/ Blood Red, Scab Red/Blood Red/Fortress Grey

Gold trim: Burnished Gold, Mithril Silver

Hair: Graveyard Earth, Bleached Bone

Horse: Codex Grey, Fortress Grey

GAMLING

Cloak: Dark Angels Green, Goblin Green

Gold trim: Burnished Gold, Mithril Silver

Hair: Snakebite Leather, Bleached Bone

Horse: Scorched Brown, Bestial Brown

Sleeves: Scab Red, Bleached Bone

HÁMA

Cloak: Catachan Green, Catachan Green/Bleached Bone

Gold trim: Shining Gold, Chainmail

Hair: Bestial Brown, Vermin Brown

Sleeves: Red Gore, Bronzed Flesh

ERKENBRAND

Cloak: Dark Angels Green, Snot Green

Gold trim: Burnished Gold, Mithril Silver

Horn: Codex Grey, Skull White

Hair: Bestial Brown, Vermin Brown

Shield: Scab Red/Blood Red, Fortress Grey

Sleeves: Red Gore, Bronzed Flesh

ROYAL GUARD

Gold trim: Burnished Gold, Mithril Silver

Sleeves: Red Gore, Bronzed Flesh

Shields: Dark Angels Green, Snot Green

ÉOWYN

Whilst Éowyn isn't in any of the scenarios, you may like to include her in Points Match games.

Dress: Shadow Grey, Space Wolves Grey

Hair: Bubonic Brown, Bleached Bone

Jerkin: Scorched Brown, Bestial Brown

Skin: Tanned Flesh, Dwarf Flesh, Elf Flesh

ROHAN BUILDINGS

The Rohirrim live in settlements of timber dwellings with low, thatched roofs. Here we show how to make a simple rectangular building, first making a card shell then applying layers of balsa wood for the timber and teddy bear fur hardened with PVA glue for the thatched roof. Once you've made one house, you can use this example to build more, adding extra details such as logs to the base or altering the design of the wooden beams attached to the roof to give their appearance more variety.

MATERIALS

- Wooden basing material
- Thick card
- 3mm balsa wood
- Teddy bear fur
- Masking tape
- Brass ring
- PVA glue
- Pencil

1. Make two end walls by cutting two rectangles measuring 80x95mm. Mark the centre of the top of the walls and cut a pitched roof 45mm from the top.

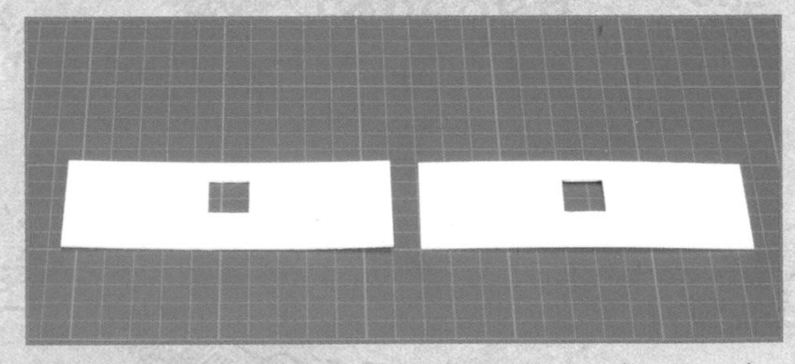

2. Make the side walls by cutting two card rectangles measuring 115x50mm. Mark out the windows and cut them out using a craft knife.

3. Assemble the building using PVA glue. Use masking tape and card triangles on the corners to add extra strength.

4. Score the balsa with lines 5mm apart using a pencil and glue it over the card. Once dry, cut out the windows and door from the inside.

5. Glue four strips of balsa to the walls. Cut the tops of the strips to match the angle of the roof and add any extra windows, shutters and doors.

6. The planking on the pitched roof is treated in the same way as the rest of the house. Just make sure that they run vertically instead of horizontally.

7. Cut a roof from card 135x150mm then fold the 150mm side in half. Using the pitched roof as a guide, cut and glue two triangular pieces of card to ensure a good fit.

8. Cut two pieces of teddy bear to fit either side of the roof and glue them in place. To cover the join at the top, cut a strip of fur 40mm wide and glue it over any gap.

9. Water down PVA glue and paint it onto the fur, thoroughly soaking it. Add some balsa strips to each end of the roof and, once dry, glue it to the house and paint as detailed below.

This campfire is made out of cocktail sticks, small stones and wire wool. Once painted, it makes a great addition to the Wrath of Rohan scenario on pages 24-25.

PAINTING A ROHAN HOUSE

The Rohan house was drybrushed using the following colours:

THATCH

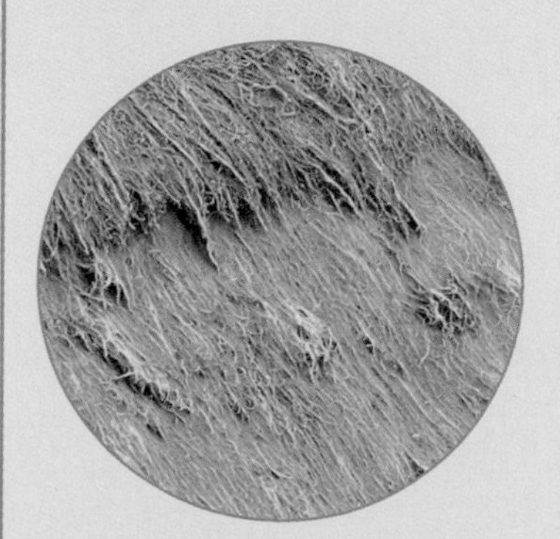

- Scorched Brown
- Scorched Brown/ Codex Grey
- Snakebite Leather
- Vomit Brown
- Bleached Bone

WOOD

- Scorched Brown
- Scorched Brown/ Codex Grey
- Bleached Bone

SCENARIO 2

THE FIRST BATTLE OF THE FORDS OF ISEN

At the fords of Isen, Saruman's betrayal is finally unmasked. A vast horde of Dunlendings and Orcs bearing the White Hand of Isengard on their shields amass on the west banks of the Isen. Théodred, heir to the throne of Rohan, guards its eastern shore and at his command are the warriors of his éored, brave and loyal Rohirrim who will sell their lives dearly to defend their lands. However, Saruman's forces will settle for slaying Théodred and undermining Rohan's leadership just as readily as winning the fords. Though he cannot know it, Théodred's doom is at hand.

PARTICIPANTS

GOOD

Théodred on horse
Erkenbrand on horse
Captain of Rohan with shield
3 Rohan Outriders
8 Warriors of Rohan with shield
8 Warriors of Rohan with throwing spear and shield
8 Warriors of Rohan with bow
8 Riders of Rohan
4 Riders of Rohan with throwing spear
1 Warrior of Rohan with banner

EVIL

Vraskû, Scout Uruk-hai Captain
Dunlending Chieftain with two-handed axe
Isengard Troll
3 Dunlending Warriors with shield
3 Dunlending Warriors with bow
3 Dunlending Warriors with two-handed weapon
8 Uruk-hai Scouts
8 Uruk-hai Scouts with shield
8 Uruk-hai Scouts with bow
3 Feral Uruk-hai
1 Warrior of Dunland with banner

LAYOUT

The scenario is played on a board 48"/112cm by 48"/112cm. The River Isen flows down the centre of the board, from short board edge to short board edge and is roughly 6"/14cm wide. In the centre of the board is the Ford of Isen, which is roughly 6"/14cm wide and counts as open ground. The land around the ford is mainly flat, with occasional clusters of rocks and brush.

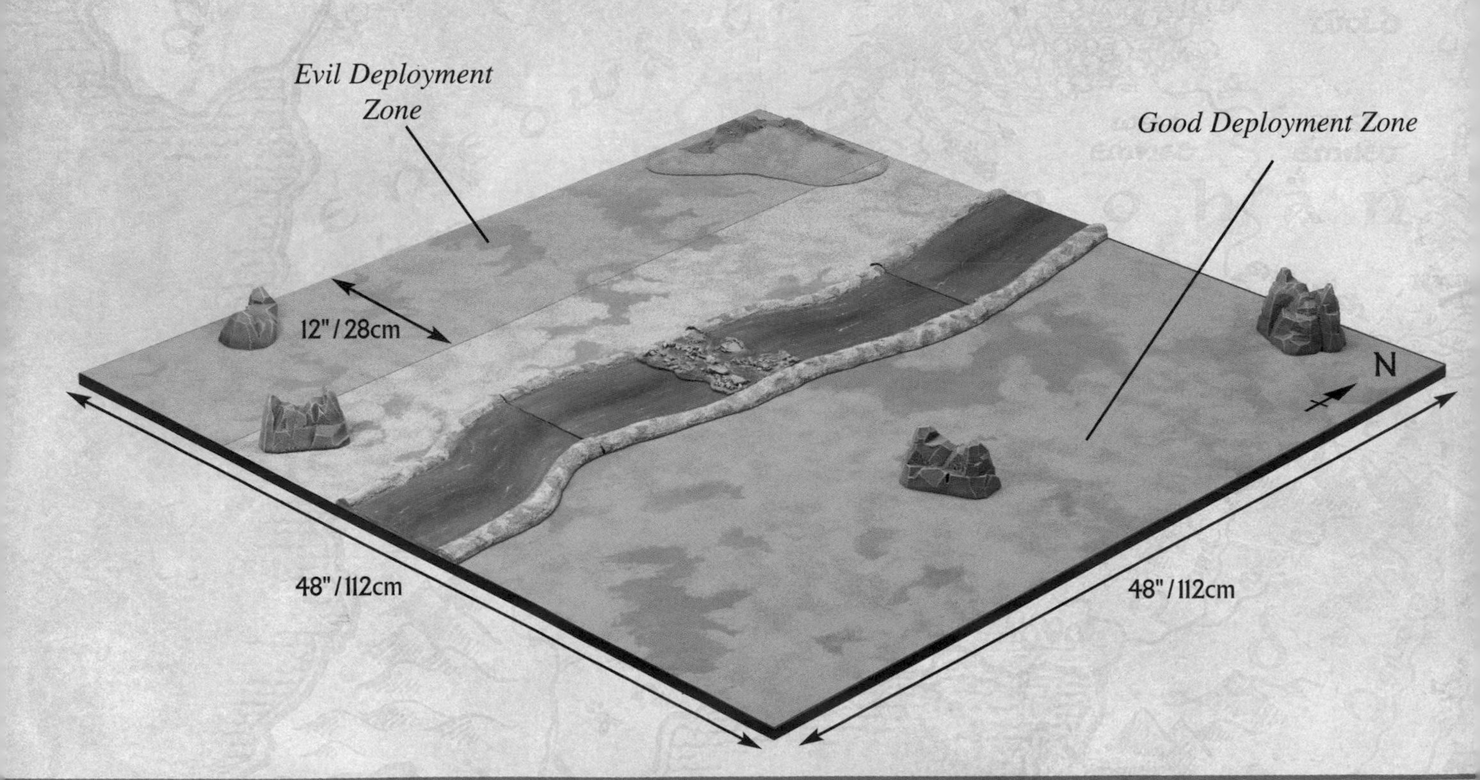

STARTING POSITIONS

The Good player deploys all of his models except Erkenbrand and the Riders of Rohan on the eastern side of the river. The remainder of the Good forces are not deployed at the start of the game, but may become available later. The Evil player deploys all of his forces within 12"/28cm of the table edge on the opposite side of the river.

OBJECTIVES

The warriors of Rohan are arrayed upon the main crossings of the River Isen and must turn back the forces of Saruman. The Good side wins if Théodred survives and there are no Evil models on the Rohan side of the river after fifteen turns. If neither of these conditions are met, the Evil side wins. If the Good side can only achieve one of the objectives, the game is a draw.

SPECIAL RULES

The River Isen. The river is in full flow and thus may not be crossed except by swimming or by using the ford. Any model that wishes to cross the Isen by any route other than the ford must make a Swimming test, as described in the main rules manual.

Death to Théodred. Saruman has demanded that his minions slay Théodred to further weaken the resolve of the Horse-lords, and no mere arrow will do. For the duration of this scenario, no Evil model may target Théodred with shooting of any kind. Such is Théodred's resolve to drive off the invaders. that he must charge an Evil model if he is within charge range at the beginning of his move.

Théodred's Doom. Though Théodred has fought in many battles, and has always come out the victor, he is ultimately ill-fated. For the duration of this scenario, every time an Evil model rolls to wound Théodred in a fight and fails, the Evil player must re-roll the dice.

Erkenbrand! Starting at the end of turn five, before players roll for priority, roll a D6. If the score is a 6, Erkenbrand and the Rohan reinforcements have arrived, and may move on from the eastern board edge at the end of the next Good Move phase. Newly arrived models may not charge, but may otherwise move as normal. If they do not arrive, roll again at the same point of turn six, with the reinforcements arriving a 5 or 6. On turn seven, the score required will be 4, 5 or 6 and will continue to be reduced by one (to a minimum of 2).

POINTS MATCH

GOOD (575 points)

Must include two Good Heroes to replace Théodred and Erkenbrand. Roughly half of the Good force takes the place of the reinforcements.

EVIL (575 points)

Must include at least one Evil Hero. No more than 33% of Evil models may carry a bow of any kind.

SCENARIO 3

THE SCOURING OF THE WESTFOLD

While the defenders at the crossing of the River Isen hold back the massed forces of Uruk-hai and Dunlendings, smaller bands of warriors bypass that crossing, heading south from Orthanc and directly into the Westfold. Plundering and destroying all in their path, their goal is to sow terror and slay the people of Rohan. Despite the swiftness and savagery of these attacks, brave men of Rohan protect the innocent civilians from Saruman's raiders. Survival for the inhabitants of the Westfold seem slim, but the Rohan Outriders are racing to their aid and together they may yet be victorious.

PARTICIPANTS

GOOD

Captain of Rohan with shield
Captain of Rohan with shield and horse
3 Rohan Outriders
4 Warriors of Rohan with shield
4 Warriors of Rohan with spear and shield
4 Warriors of Rohan with bow
1 Warrior of Rohan with banner
1 Rider of Rohan with banner

EVIL

Dunlending Chieftain with two-handed axe
Uruk-hai Captain with two-handed axe
3 Dunlending Warriors with shield
3 Dunlending Warriors with two-handed axe
3 Dunlending Warriors with bow
8 Uruk-hai Scouts with shield
4 Uruk-hai Scouts with Orc bow
1 Dunlending Warrior with a banner

LAYOUT

This scenario is played on a 48"/112cm x 48"/112cm table, representing a typical village within the Westfold. Place three Rohan houses within 12"/28cm of the centre of the board (see map). There are also two small hills, one small wood (of about three trees) and one large wood (of about five trees).

STARTING POSITIONS

The Good player places the Captain on foot and Warriors of Rohan anywhere within 6"/14cm of any of the houses. The Evil player then positions his models touching any board edge, with no more than eight models on any one edge. The Rohan Outriders, the mounted Captain and the Rider of Rohan with banner do not start the game in play, but will become available as reserves later (see special rules).

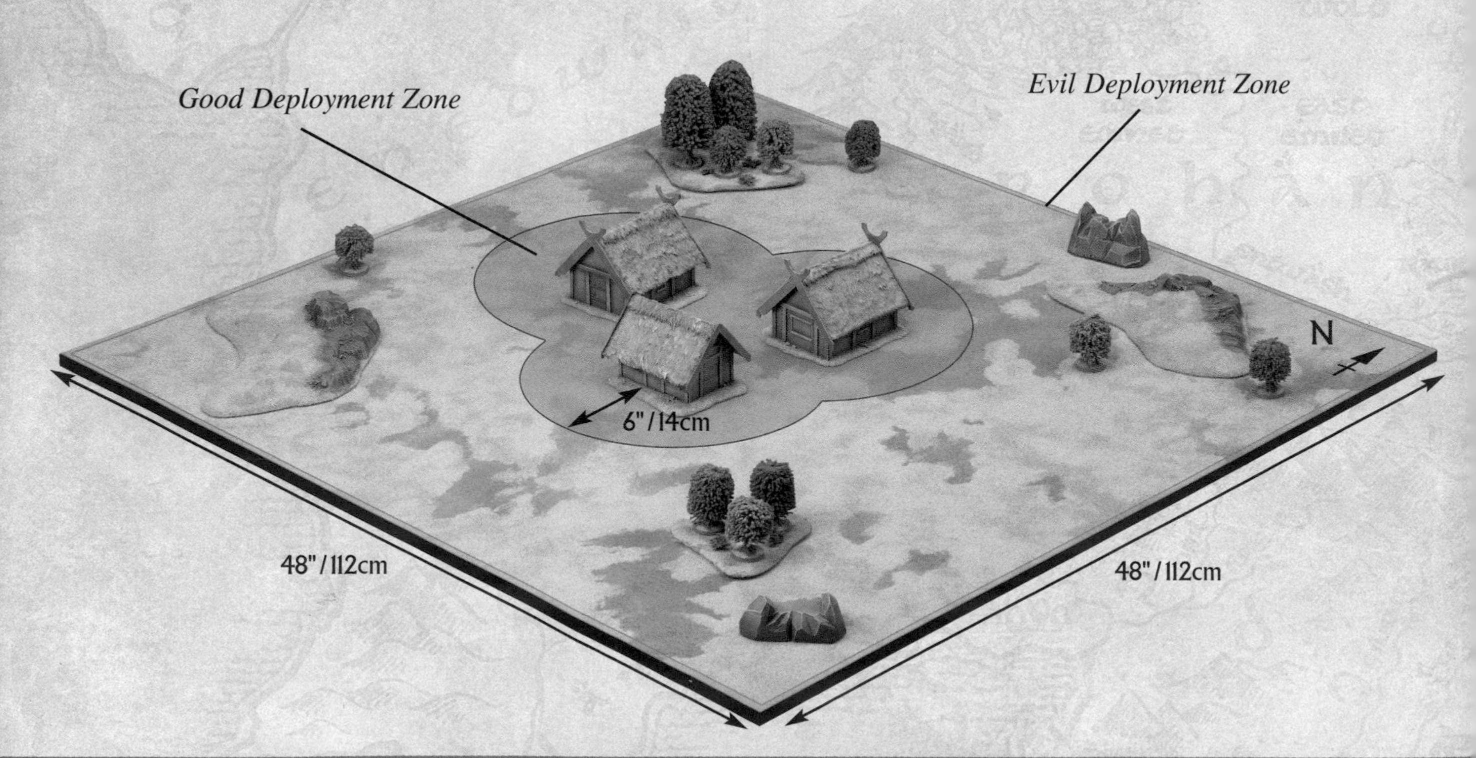

OBJECTIVES

The Rohirrim have mustered to defend the Westfold against the Dunlendings and Saruman's Uruk-hai. The Good player wins this scenario if at least two out of the three houses survive the game. The Evil player wins if his force can destroy all three of the Rohan houses by setting fire to them. If two houses are destroyed, the game is a draw. The game will end if all three houses are destroyed, or the raiders are killed.

SPECIAL RULES

Burning houses. The Dunlendings and Uruk-hai carry torches and oils to set alight the houses and barns of the Rohirrim. At the beginning of the Fight phase, any Evil model in base contact with a Rohan house who has not used a missile weapon and is not engaged in a fight may attempt to set the house alight. Roll a D6; on a 5 or a 6 the house is set ablaze. Additional Evil models can help set the house alight. For each additional Evil model helping, reduce the score needed by 1. A roll of 1 always fails though.

Once it is on fire, place a counter beside the house to show it is burning. Each turn that the building remains on fire, add another counter at the end of the Fight phase on the score of a 4,5 or 6. Once a building has six counters, the fire has consumed it, and the building is destroyed.

Good models can attempt to beat out the flames before they can fully take hold. At the beginning of the Fight phase, any Good model in base contact with a Rohan house who has not used a missile weapon and is not engaged in a fight may attempt to set beat out the flames. Roll a D6; on the score of a 5 or 6 remove one counter from the burning building. If this reduces the number of counters to 0, the flames have been extinguished completely. Additional Good models can help beat out the flames. For each additional Good model helping, reduce the score needed by 1. A roll of 1 always fails though.

Reinforcements. The Rohan Outriders have been dispatched to reinforce the Westfold and are racing towards the scene of the battle. From turn two onwards, make a roll, before rolling for priority, to see if they arrive. On turn two the reinforcements will arrive on the score of a 6. If they do not arrive, add 1 to the dice roll each turn until they do (a roll of 1 always fails though). When they arrive, reinforcements enter play from the east board edge, as shown on the map. They may not charge on the turn they arrive, but may otherwise act normally.

Desperate defence. The Rohirrim defending the village know full well that the lives of many innocents, possibly their families and friends, are at stake if they cannot defeat the invaders. The Good side does not have to test for being Broken in this scenario.

POINTS MATCH

GOOD (300 points)

Must include at least two Heroes, none of which may have more than 2 Wounds. Roughly a third of the force takes the place of the reinforcements, including a Hero.

EVIL (300 points)

Must include at least one Hero, none of which may have more than 2 Wounds. No more than a third of the force may carry bows of any kind, and no Evil models may ride steeds of any kind.

SCENARIO 4

THE WRATH OF ROHAN

Even as Merry and Pippin are borne towards Isengard by the servants of Saruman, the Riders of Éomer scour the plains of Rohan for intruders, slaughtering all enemies that they find. By chance Éomer and his warriors happen upon Uglúk and his band. Even as the Rohirrim charge towards the unsuspecting Orcs, Merry and Pippin struggle with their bonds, desperately trying to flee from their captors. Seeing the attack as the diversion they need, the Hobbits prepare to flee into the nearby woods, hoping that they will not fall foul of the chaos of battle.

PARTICIPANTS

GOOD

Meriadoc Brandybuck with Elven cloak
Peregrin Took with Elven cloak
Éomer with horse
Captain of Rohan with horse and shield
3 Rohan Outriders
12 Riders of Rohan
6 Riders of Rohan with throwing spear
1 Rider of Rohan with banner

EVIL

Uglúk
Grishnákh
8 Uruk-hai Scouts
8 Uruk-hai Scouts with shield
8 Uruk-hai Scouts with bow
8 Orcs with shield
8 Orcs with spear
4 Orcs with bow
4 Orcs with two-handed weapon

LAYOUT

This scenario is played on a 48"/112cm x 48"/112cm table, representing the edge of Fangorn Forest. The northern edge of the board is heavily wooded – represent this with two small woods (of about three trees) and one large wood (of about five trees) and as many other trees as you can place within 12"/28cm of the Fangorn edge (see map). There are also two small hills and several rocky outcrops on the board, as well as a campfire in the centre.

STARTING POSITIONS

The Evil player places all of his models within 12"/28cm of the centre of the board. The Good player then positions Merry and Pippin anywhere within 6"/14cm of the centre of the board. The Rohirrim force is divided into two equal halves, and split between the east and west edges, within 6"/14cm of the table edge.

OBJECTIVES

The Good player has two objectives. Firstly, the Hobbits must escape into Fangorn, by moving off the Fangorn board edge. Secondly, Éomer, enraged by the Orcs trespassing on his land, must wipe out all the Evil models. If the Good player only achieves one of these objectives, the game is a draw.

For the Evil player to win, he must have control of the Hobbits and reduce the Riders of Rohan to 25% of their starting numbers.

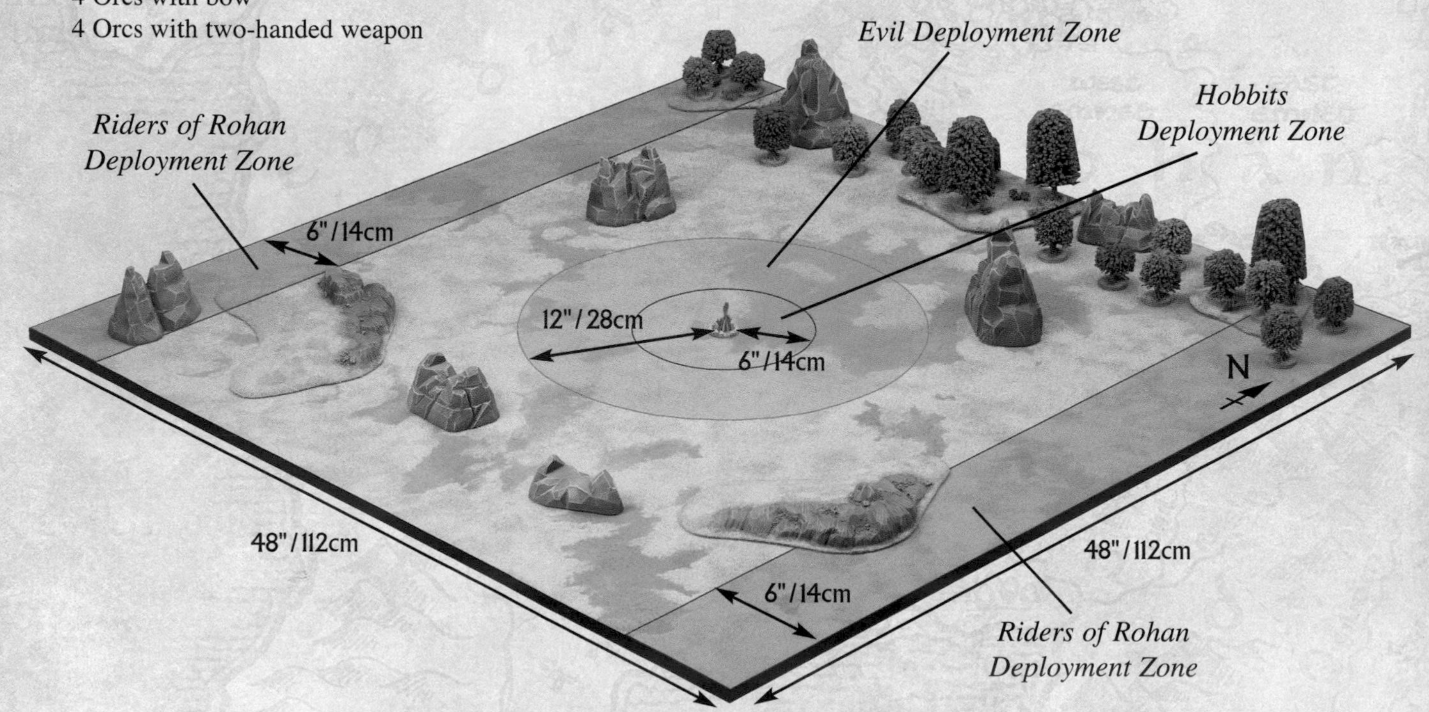

SPECIAL RULES

Controlling the Hobbits. At the start of the game the Hobbits are presumed to have slipped their bonds and are ready to make a break for it. While the Hobbits remain within 6"/14cm of the fire, they cannot be charged or attacked in any way and may never be targeted with shooting. Merry and Pippin may move and fight as normal, but if they move beyond this, they may be attacked as normal. If the Hobbits lose a fight, the Orcs will not slay them (except Grishnákh, see below), instead they will be taken prisoner, at which point each captured Hobbit will count as a light object (see the main rules manual) and are considered to be controlled. Should the captor be forced to release a controlled Hobbit, it may act as normal from that point onward.

Fleeing Hobbits. Merry and Pippin are terrified, and ready to flee for their lives. They do not take Courage tests (of any kind) in this scenario. In addition, Merry and Pippin may only charge an Evil model that is already engaged with his fellow Hobbit.

Grishnákh. Unwilling to fall into line with the rest of the Orcs, Grishnákh is quite happy to take Hobbit corpses back to his master. If at any point the Hobbits are more than 6"/14cm from the centre of the board, Grishnákh may attack and wound them as normal. If he kills the Hobbits, they count as 'controlled' at the end of the scenario.

POINTS MATCH

GOOD (500 points)

Must include two models to take the place of Merry and Pippin (1 Wound maximum). The remainder of the force takes the place of Éomer and his warriors.

EVIL (475 points)

Must include two Heroes, with no more than 2 Wounds, one of which takes the place of Grishnákh. No more than a third of the force may carry bows, and no Evil models may be mounted.

ENTS

The Ents are the huge tree herders who attack Isengard after their forests are destroyed by Orcs. Powerful adversaries, Treebeard first appears in Alone in Fangorn (scenario 5) whilst other Ents appear in The Last March of the Ents (scenario 8).

TREEBEARD

Bark: Scorched Brown, Graveyard Earth, Bleached Bone, Brown Ink

Leaves: Dark Angels Green, Catachan Green, Dark Green Ink

Trees come in many different colours and the best reference is to take a look in your garden. To get you started, below are two alternate palettes.

SILVER BARK

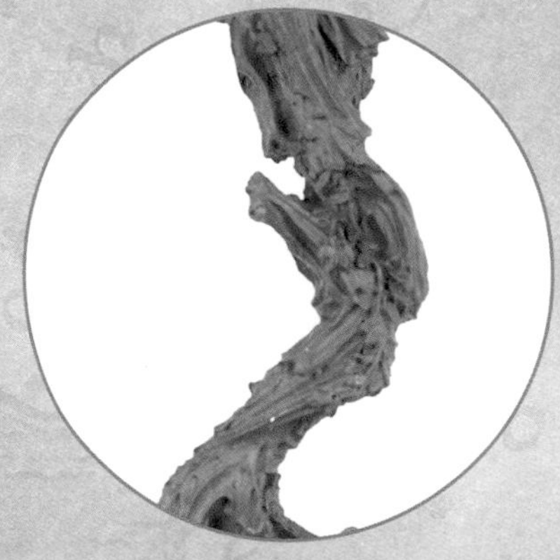

Paint on a basecoat of Graveyard Earth.

Next, apply a Brown Ink wash.

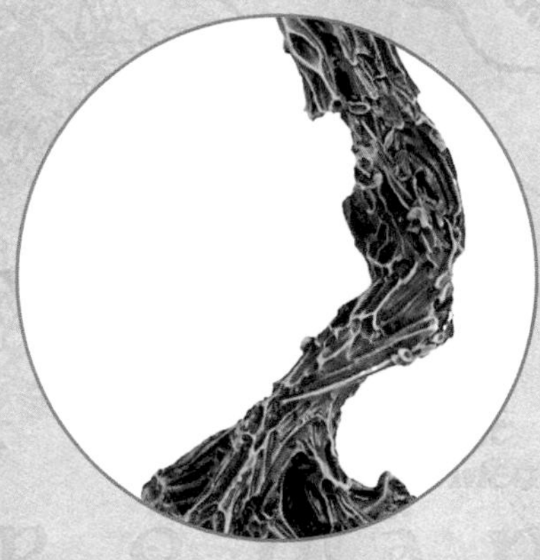

Once thoroughly dry, drybrush with Fortress Grey.

OAK BARK

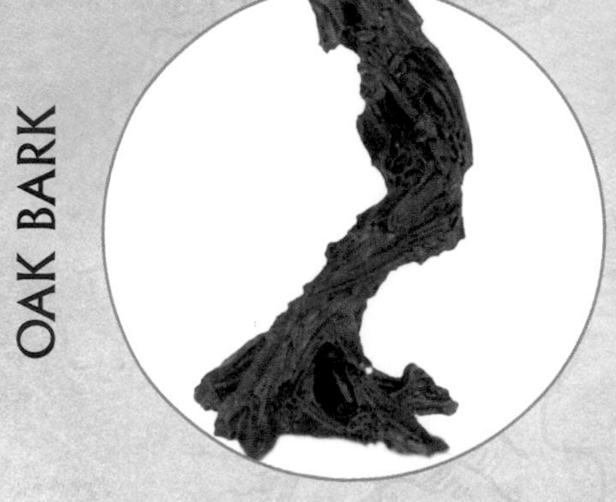

First apply a heavy drybrush of Scorched Brown over a Chaos Black undercoat.

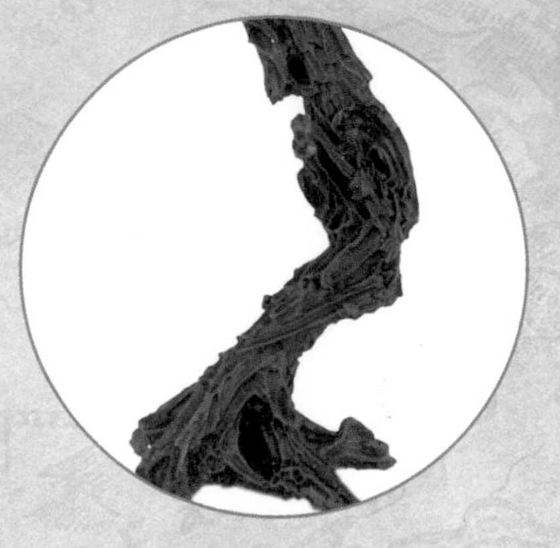

Then apply a drybrush of Bestial Brown.

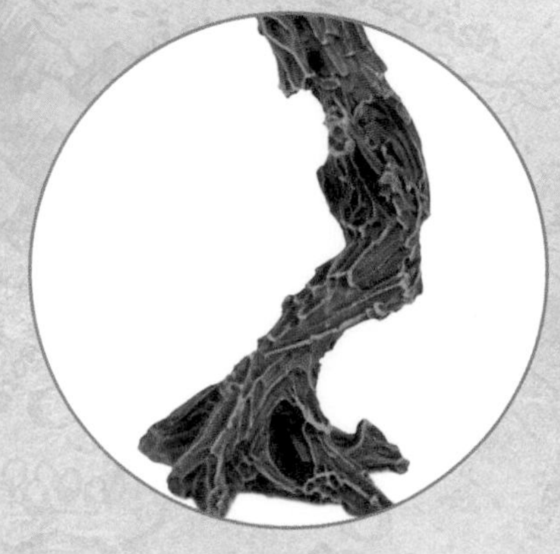

Finally highlight with a light drybrush of Vomit Brown.

UNDERGROWTH AND ROUGH GROUND

Under the thick canopy of leaves, the forest floor of Fangorn is a mass of dense roots and bushes. Areas of rough, uneven ground can be built to represent this on the table top. There are a number of materials that look like long grass and roots, and these can also be applied to the bases of larger models, such as the Ents.

MATERIALS

Wooden basing material	Clump foliage
5mm thick foamboard	Model hedge
Ready-mix filler	Green flock
Gravel	Static grass
Stones	PVA glue
Sand	

1. First cut a wooden base and bevel the edges.

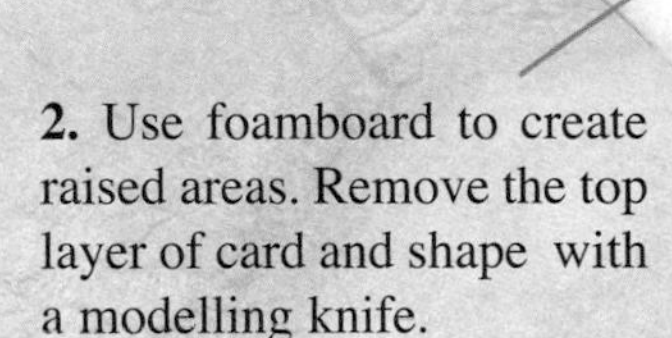

2. Use foamboard to create raised areas. Remove the top layer of card and shape with a modelling knife.

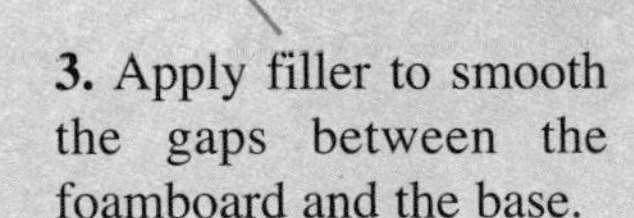

3. Apply filler to smooth the gaps between the foamboard and the base.

4. Glue small stones and patches of gravel onto the mounds.

5. Paint and flock the base to match the rest of your hills. Attach patches of clump foliage and small pieces of model hedge to finish.

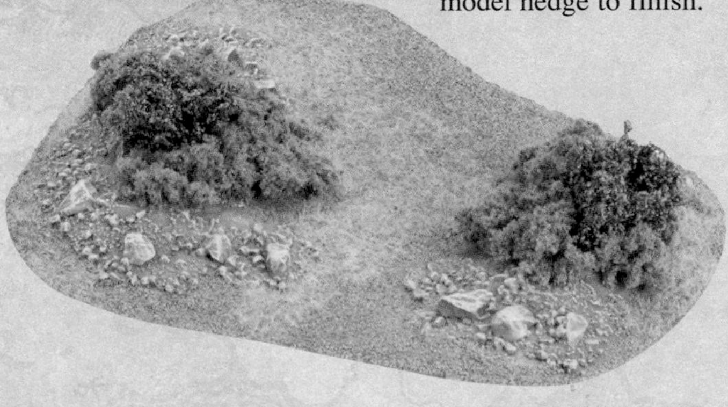

APPLYING UNDERGROWTH TO BASES

Pieces of clump foliage and model hedge can also be used to decorate bases of large models. Ents look particularly effective when their bases are finished in this way.

SCENARIO 5

ALONE IN FANGORN

Their daring escape from Uglúk and Grishnákh successful, Merry and Pippin flee into the depths of Fangorn, hotly pursued by the remnants of Uglúk's Orc band. Alone, they have no chance against a band of ravening Orcs, and should they be caught, the Hobbits' fate will be painful and their death slow. But Fangorn is a mysterious place, and there are things far stranger and more deadly than mere Orcs living beneath its leaves and boughs.

PARTICIPANTS

GOOD

Meriadoc Brandybuck with Elven cloak
Peregrin Took with Elven cloak
Treebeard

EVIL

1 Orc with shield
1 Orc with spear
1 Orc with Orc bow
1 Orc with two-handed weapon
1 Uruk-hai Scout
1 Uruk-hai Scout with shield
1 Uruk-hai Scout with Orc bow

LAYOUT

This scenario is played on a 24"/56cm x 24"/56cm table, representing a small clearing of the mighty Fangorn Forest. Two small forests (of about three trees each) and one large forest (of about five trees) should be placed on the board as shown. Additionally, as many other trees as are available should be placed on the board, with these extra trees no closer than 3"/8cm to each other. Two small hills and several areas of difficult ground should also be placed on the board (see map).

STARTING POSITIONS

Merry and Pippin start the scenario touching the centre of the east board edge (see map). The Orcs and Uruk-hai all start deployed within 6"/14cm of any corner of the map, as shown. Treebeard is placed in the centre of the board.

"The Hobbits turned and fled deep into the shadows of the wood."

The Two Towers

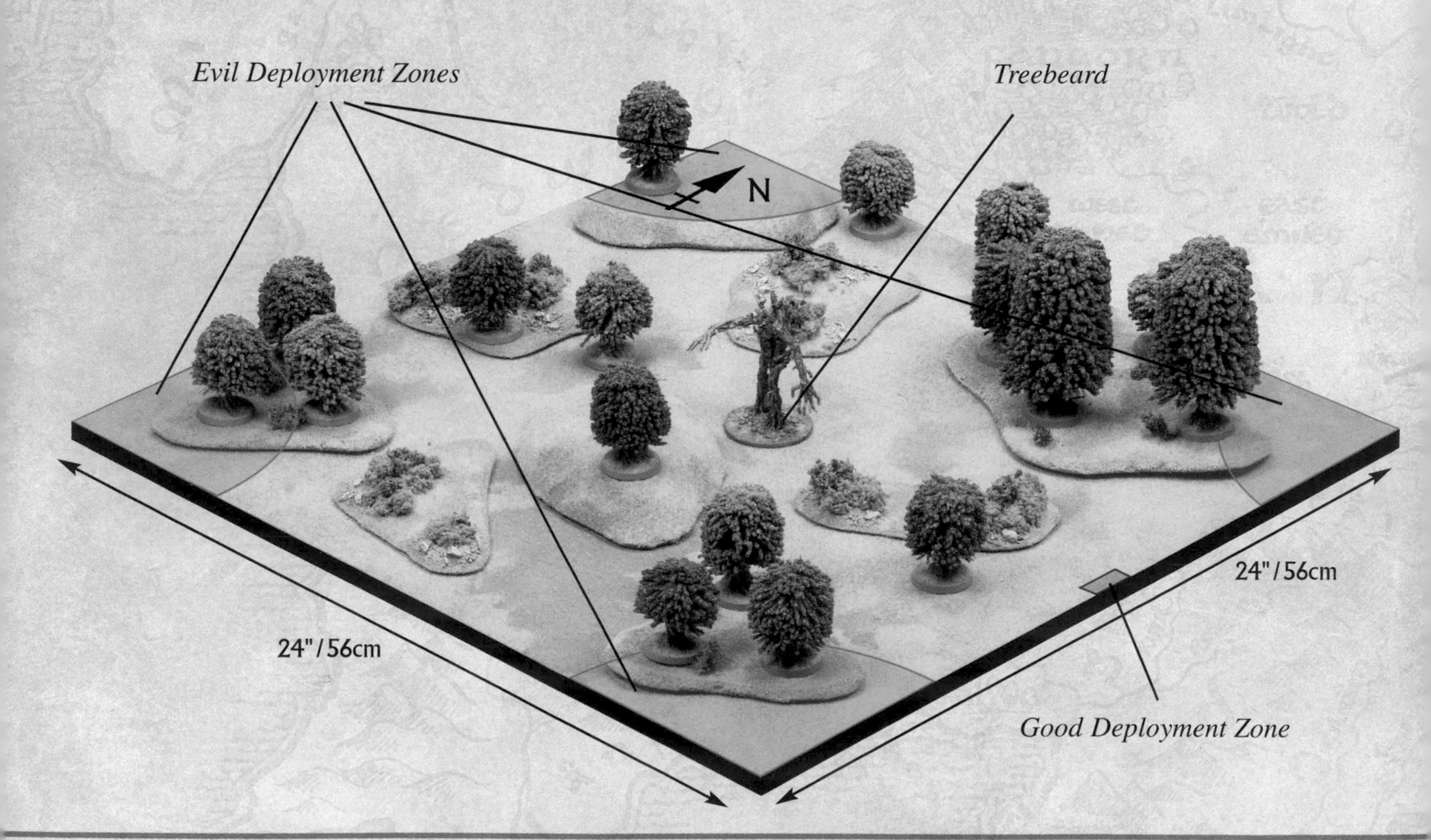

OBJECTIVE

With the rest of their raiding party slaughtered, the Orcish warriors chasing Merry and Pippin are now quite happy to slay the two Hobbits and drag their corpses back to their master.

The Good player wins if Merry and Pippin survive the scenario. The Evil player wins if both Merry and Pippin are slain. If only one Hobbit is killed, the game is a draw. The game ends if both Hobbits, or all the Orcs are slain.

SPECIAL RULES

Panicked Orcs. The Orcs know that only bringing the Hobbits back to their master will save them from harsh punishment. At the start of the game, all Evil models follow the rules given for Sentries, as explained on page 73 of the main rules manual.

Slumbering Treebeard. Treebeard is deep in sleep, and has no idea of the Hobbits' plight. He is, however, the tallest tree in this part of the forest, and his sturdy branches are the perfect place for the Hobbits to hide. If the Hobbits are in base contact with Treebeard they will wake him on the score of a 4+ at the start of the End phase. Once woken, Treebeard acts normally from the following Good Move phase onward. Until woken, Treebeard cannot move or fight, has no control zone and will not alert sentries if they are within 4"/10cm at the end of their move.

Scenario Note. If you wish to play this scenario as it appears in the film, simply swap all the Evil models given in the scenario participants for Grishnákh.

POINTS MATCH

GOOD (225 points)

Must include 3 models, two of which may not have more than 1 Wound. The most expensive of these models takes the place of Treebeard.

EVIL (50 points)

Force must be composed of either a single Hero with no more than 2 Wounds, or entirely of Warriors that have 1 Wound each. No more than a third of the Evil models may carry bows, and none may ride steeds of any kind.

WARG RIDERS

The Warg Riders are unleashed by Saruman against King Théoden's people as they race to Helm's Deep. They are cruel warriors mounted on vicious Wargs who take part in the Warg Attack (scenario 6) and the Second Battle of the Fords of Isen (scenario 7).

WARG

- **Skin:** Chaos Black, Codex Grey
- **Teeth:** Scorched Brown, Bleached Bone
- **Tongue:** Red Gore, Red Gore/Bleached Bone

To paint the Orcs, refer to the colour palettes on page 9.

WARG FUR

Heavily drybrush the fur Scorched Brown.

Then drybrush with Bestial Brown.

Finally, apply a light drybrush of Snakebite Leather.

SHARKU

The leader of the Warg Riders is the venomous Sharku. His light coloured skin is quite different from the rest of his Warg Riders, making him stand out.

SHARKU'S SKIN

Paint a basecoat mix of Vermin Brown and Brown Ink.

Highlight with a mix of Vermin Brown and Skull White.

Add Skull White to the previous mix for the final highlight.

WARRIORS OF DUNLAND

The Dunlendings are sworn enemies of Rohan and, together with Saruman, seek its downfall. They are courageous warriors and take part in The First Battle of the Fords of Isen (scenario 2), the Scouring of the Westfold (scenario 3) and The Battle For Helm's Deep (scenarios 13-17).

WARRIORS OF DUNLAND

- **Cloth:** Scab Red, Blood Red
- **Leather:** Scorched Brown, Bestial Brown
- **Metal:** Boltgun Metal, Black/Brown Ink, Chainmail
- **Skin:** Tanned Flesh, Dwarf Flesh
- **Trim:** Brazen Brass, Mithril Silver
- **Hair:** See the Rohan painting guides

ARMOUR

Paint the armour Boltgun Metal.

Apply a mix of Black Ink and Brown Ink.

Finish off by drybrushing with Chainmail.

WILD MEN OF DUNLAND

The Wild Men of Dunland were cast out of Rohan in ages past, and their lands were taken by the Rohirrim. While they aren't listed in any of the scenarios, you may like to include them in Points Match games.

WILD MEN

- **Cloth:** Codex Grey, Fortress Grey
- **Fur:** Shadow Grey, Space Wolves Grey
- **Hair colours:** Codex Grey or Scorched Brown or Bestial Brown
- **Leather:** Scorched Brown, Bestial Brown
- **Skin:** Tanned Flesh, Dwarf Flesh
- **Wood:** Scorched Brown, Bestial Brown

SCENARIO 6

WARG ATTACK

King Théoden has commanded that the city of Edoras be emptied and that his people make their way to the ancient refuge of Helm's Deep, a journey that is both long and fraught with peril. Saruman's forces scour the lands of Rohan, looking to ambush and slay Théoden's people before the Rohirrim can reach safety. Háma and Gamling chance upon a group of enemy scouts and the full fury of the Warg Riders looks set to descend upon them. King Théoden, Aragorn, Legolas and Gimli rally the Riders of Rohan to intercept the Wolves of Isengard. Led by Sharku, the Warg Riders will offer no mercy to any they catch, and battle is joined in a furious clash of fangs and blades.

PARTICIPANTS

GOOD

Aragorn with Andúril, Elven cloak and horse
Legolas with Elven cloak and horse
Gimli with Elven cloak
Théoden, King of Rohan with horse
Gamling, Captain of Rohan with horse
Captain of Rohan with horse
4 Riders of Rohan
2 Riders of Rohan with throwing spear

EVIL

Sharku, Warg Rider Captain
6 Warg Riders
6 Warg Riders with throwing spear
6 Warg Riders with bow

LAYOUT

The scenario is played on a board 48"/112cm by 48"/112cm. This scenario takes place in the White Mountains, and the ground is strewn with rocky outcrops and two rocky hills – one in the south-eastern corner, one in the south-western corner.

STARTING POSITIONS

The Good player places Gamling and the Captain of Rohan within 3"/8cm of the centre of the board. Legolas begins the game in the centre of the south-eastern hill with Gimli as a passenger on his horse. The Evil player then places six Warg Riders anywhere on the board, but no closer that 10"/24cm to any Good model. The remaining models are not deployed now, but will become available as the game progresses.

"It is howling with wolf voices."

Aragorn, The Fellowship of The Ring

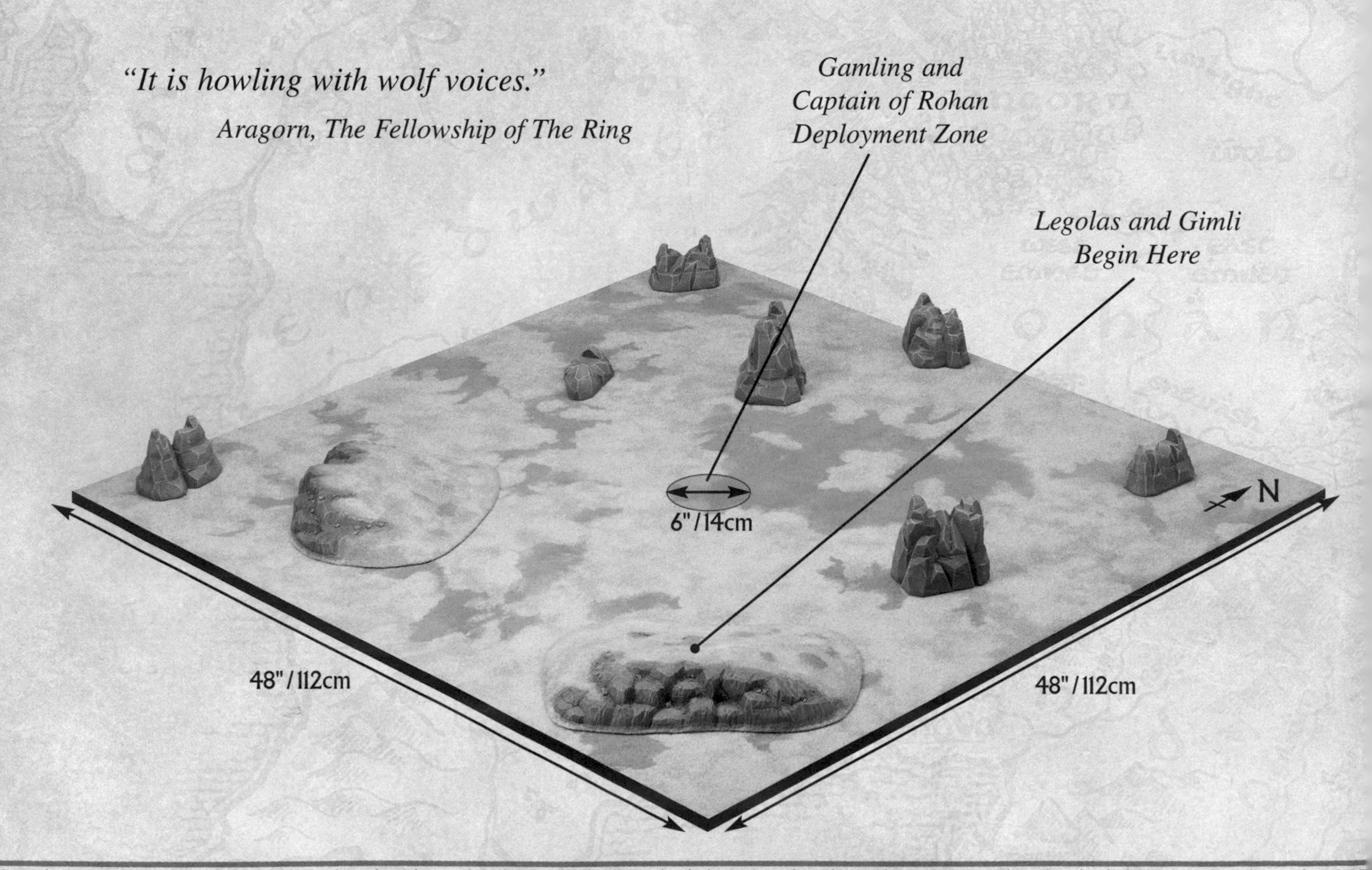

OBJECTIVES

The Warg Riders soon see who they are up against and know that if they were to slay any of these mighty heroes, Saruman will richly reward them. The Evil player wins if he is able to slay any two Good Heroes by the end of turn 8. The Good player wins if he manages to prevent this.

SPECIAL RULES

Ambush: The Warg Riders have surprised Gamling and the Captain, and caught them flat-footed. This means that, for the purposes of this scenario, the Good player does not automatically get priority in the first turn, it must be rolled for as normal. If the player's dice scores are tied, re-roll the dice until one player wins priority. In addition, no heroic moves may be called by the Good player in the first turn.

To battle!: As the cry goes up that battle is joined, warriors rush to the battlefield to fight. From turn two onwards, at the end of each player's Move phase, roll a D6 for each model not yet deployed. On a 4, 5 or 6, that model may enter play. Good models move on from the eastern board edge and Evil models may move on from any board edge. Models that arrive in this way may not charge, but may otherwise move as normal.

Reinforcements: Roll a dice for each Evil warrior killed during the course of this scenario (not those removed due to a failed Courage test). On a 4, 5 or 6, place them with any models not yet deployed, where they may re-enter play, as described above.

POINTS MATCH

Good (650 points)
Must include at least four Heroes. All models in must be mounted on steeds. Select two Heroes to take the place of Gamling and the Captain or Rohan.

Evil (350 points)
Must include a single Hero. All Evil models must be mounted and no more than a third of the Evil force may be equipped with bows of any kind.

SCENARIO 7

THE SECOND BATTLE OF THE FORDS OF ISEN

Orcs, Dunlendings and the wolves of Isengard gather to make war on King Théoden's people. Though the forces of Evil have been turned back from the strategic crossing of the Fords of Isen once already, the cost has been high. Once again the enemy attempts to force a crossing, but the warriors of the Westfold resolve not to yield without a fight. As night falls and the vast size of the army arrayed before them becomes apparent, it is clear that this attack cannot be stopped, only delayed. Can the Rohirrim hold out long enough to allow Théoden to complete his muster at Helm's Deep...

PARTICIPANTS

GOOD

Erkenbrand (on foot)
Captain of Rohan with shield
Captain of Rohan mounted on horse
5 Rohan Royal Guard with horse and throwing spear
6 Rohan Royal Guard with throwing spear
4 Riders of Rohan with throwing spear
8 Riders of Rohan
8 Warriors of Rohan with bow
8 Warriors of Rohan with shield
8 Warriors of Rohan with throwing spear and shield
1 Warrior of Rohan with banner

EVIL

1 Dunlending Chieftain with two-handed axe
Vraskû, Scout Uruk-hai Captain
Uruk-hai Shaman
5 Dunlending Warriors with two-handed axe
5 Dunlending Warriors with bow
5 Dunlending Warriors with hand weapon and shield
8 Scout Uruk-hai with Orc bow
8 Scout Uruk-hai with shield
3 Feral Uruk-hai
6 Warg Riders with throwing spear
6 Warg Riders with shield
1 Isengard Troll
1 Dunlending Warrior carries a banner.

LAYOUT

The scenario is played on a board 48"/112cm by 48"/112cm. The River Isen flows down the centre of the board, from short board edge to short board edge and is roughly 6"/14cm wide. In the centre of the board is the Ford of Isen, which is roughly 6"/14cm wide and counts as open ground. The land around the ford is mainly flat, with the occasional clusters of rocks and brush.

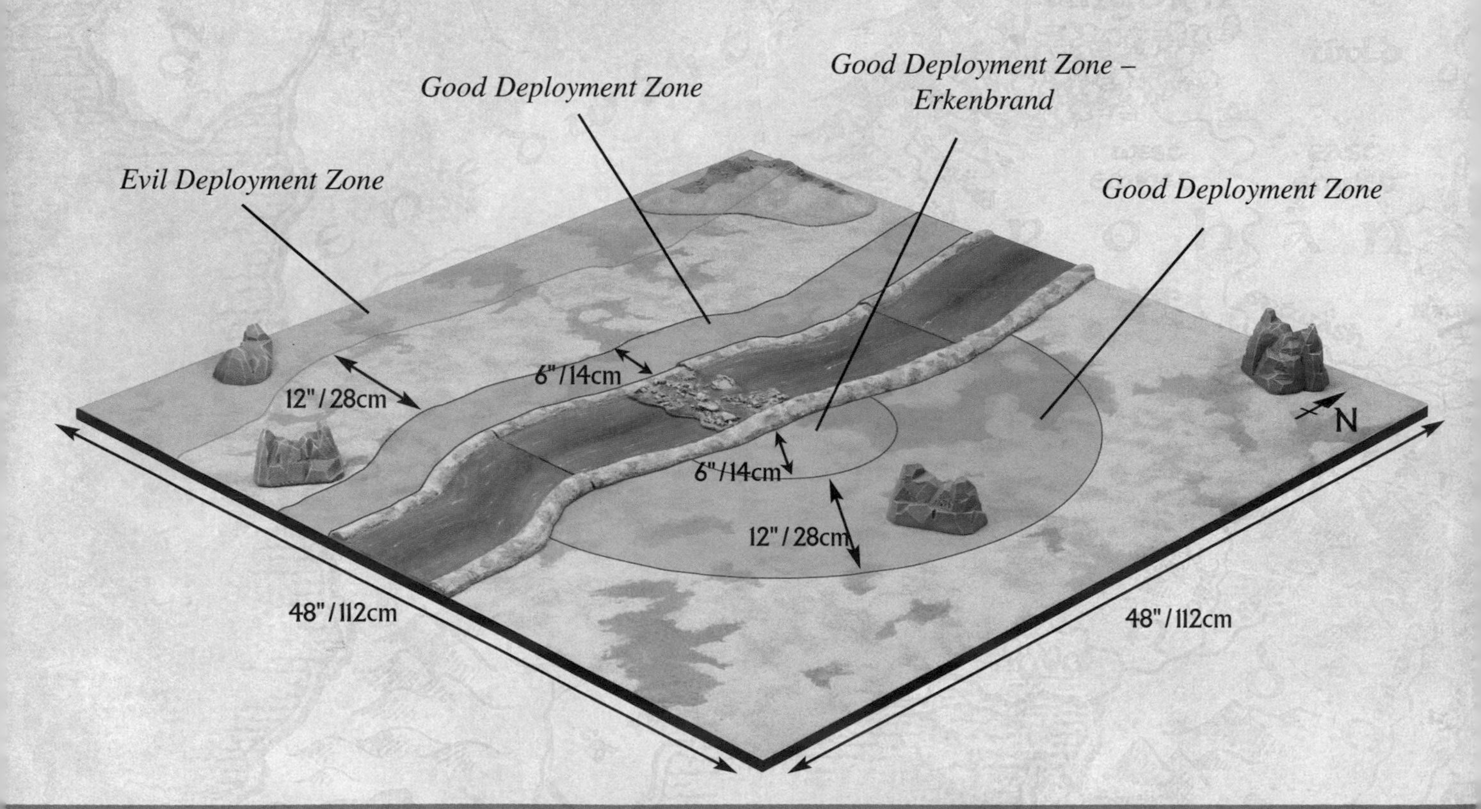

STARTING POSITIONS

The Good player deploys the Captain of Rohan on foot and the Warriors of Rohan with shields on the western bank of the river no further than 6"/14cm from the riverbank. Erkenbrand is deployed within 6"/14cm of the ford on the eastern riverbank and the Rohan Royal Guard on foot and the Warriors of Rohan armed with bows and Warriors of Rohan with throwing spears must be deployed within 12"/28cm of him. The mounted Captain of Rohan and all the mounted warriors are not deployed on the battlefield, but will become available later in the game. The Evil player then deploys all his models except the Warg Riders anywhere on the western bank of the river, but no closer than 12"/28cm to any Good models.

OBJECTIVES

To win, the Evil player must reduce the Good force to less than 25% of its starting numbers (12 models in the given scenario participants) by the end of turn ten. If he fails to do this, the Good player wins.

SPECIAL RULES

The River Isen. Saruman's forces have attacked when the river is at its shallowest, and thus the river merely counts as difficult ground. Crossing the river via the Fords of Isen incurs no movement penalty.

To the rescue! At the beginning of the Good player's Move phase on turn three, roll a D6. On a roll of a 4, 5 or 6, the Captain of Rohan on horseback and the remainder of the Good force moves onto the table from the northern board edge of the east bank. If the roll is a 1, 2 or 3, roll again at the beginning of each of the Good player's Move phases until they arrive. Newly arrived models may not charge, but may otherwise act normally.

Outflanked. At the beginning of the Evil player's Move phase on turn 4, roll a D6. On a 4, 5 or 6, the Warg Riders move onto the table from the eastern board edge. If the roll is a 1, 2 or 3, roll again at the beginning of each of the Evil player's Move phases until they arrive. Newly arrived models may not charge, but may otherwise act normally.

None shall pass! The warriors of the Westfold are determined to hold the Fords of Isen at all costs, but the sudden arrival of enemies in their rear deals a crushing blow to their morale. Until the arrival of the Warg Riders, all Good models automatically pass any Courage tests they are required to make. As soon as the Warg Riders arrive, all Good models take Courage tests as normal.

POINTS MATCH

Good (600 points)

Must include three Heroes. Up to half the Good force may be mounted on steeds. No more than a third of the Good models may be armed with bows.

Evil (775 points)

Must include three Heroes. No more than a third of the Evil force may be equipped with bows or crossbows.

PAINTING

SARUMAN AND GRÍMA

Saruman the Wizard has allied himself with Mordor against the Free Peoples. Aided by his henchman Gríma Wormtongue, Saruman musters a huge army of Uruk-hai to destroy Rohan. While these two aren't in any of the scenarios, you may like to include them in Points Match games.

SARUMAN

Beard: Fortress Grey, Skull White

Orb: Skull White, 'Ardcoat

Skin: Tanned Flesh, Dwarf Flesh

Staff: Chaos Black, Codex Grey

GRÍMA

Cloak: Chaos Black, Codex Grey

Fur: Graveyard Earth, Bleached Bone

Skin: Dwarf Flesh, Elf Flesh/Skull White

Sleeves: Graveyard Earth

SARUMAN'S CLOAK

Start by applying a mix of Bestial Brown, Codex Grey and Bleached Bone.

Shade this layer with a mix of Bestial Brown and Codex Grey.

Add more Bleached Bone to the original mix and highlight the cloth.

Apply thin Bleached Bone highlights on top.

Mix Bleached Bone and Skull White and apply as final highlights.

Due to their prominence in the story of The Two Towers, Saruman and Gríma are a great addition to any collection.

ORTHANC SCAFFOLDS

The torn and ripped landscape at Orthanc is covered in ramshackle mine workings and lifting gear used by Saruman's Orcs to excavate the land for its iron ore. These structures are built from sheets and strips of balsa wood, with details made from plasticard and twine. You can use the same approach to make more of these models and, with a little imagination, alter their shapes to create new ones.

MATERIALS

Wooden basing material
3mm balsa wood
String
Uruk-hai ladders
Gravel
Stones
Sand
PVA glue

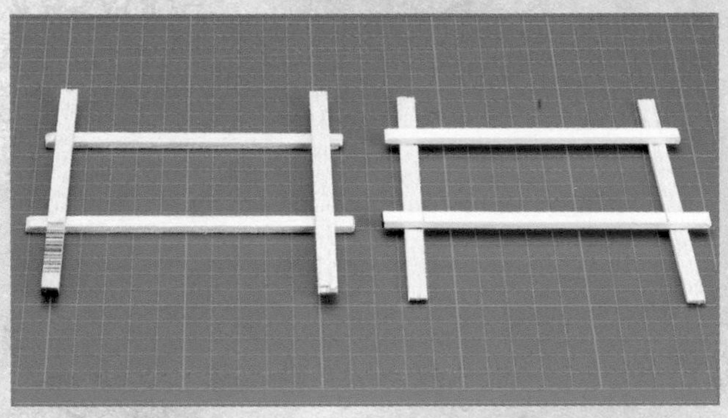

1. Cut eight strips of balsa, approximately 6" long, and make two frames.

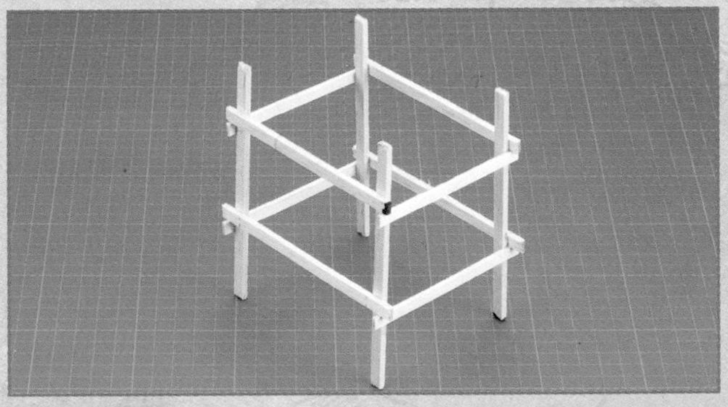

2. Cut four more strips and use these to join the two frames together.

3. Add a couple of balsa floor sections, scoring the wood with a pen to make separate planks.

4. Add ladders and simple winches from balsa strips, lashed together with string. Paint to match your Rohan building.

Making your own scaffolds

Once you've made one of these scaffolds, you can use the same approach to make more – try to give them a different look by changing the model's size and shape as well as altering the details.

THE LAST MARCH OF THE ENTS

Having escaped Grishnákh and fallen into the care of Treebeard, Merry and Pippin spend several days resting and recovering in Fangorn. Their time is not wasted though, for while they dwell amongst the Ents they warn them of Saruman's plans. Treebeard, first amongst the Ents, summons his kin to an Entmoot, a great gathering of tree shepherds, where they can decide what action to take against the White Wizard of Orthanc. Though some, like Quickbeam, are swift to reach a decision, only after three nights do the Ents finally resolve to march on Isengard. Not since ages past have Orcs so despoiled their forest, and the Ents stride towards Orthanc to hew its stones, break its doors and end Saruman's destructive ways.

PARTICIPANTS

GOOD

Treebeard
3 Ents

EVIL

Uruk-hai Captain with shield
Orc Captain with shield
Isengard Troll
5 Uruk-hai Warriors with pike
5 Uruk-hai Warriors with shield
3 Uruk-hai Warriors with crossbow
3 Uruk-hai Berserkers
3 Feral Uruk-hai
4 Orcs with shield
4 Orcs with spear
2 Orcs with bow
2 Orcs with two-handed weapon
1 Uruk-hai Warrior with banner
1 Orc Warrior with banner

LAYOUT

This scenario is played on a 48"/112cm x 24"/56cm table, representing the Circle of Isengard. Three of Saruman's structures are placed on the board at least 12"/28cm away from each other. In addition, two small rocky outcrops and two large rocky outcrops are placed on the board as well as three fissures (see map).

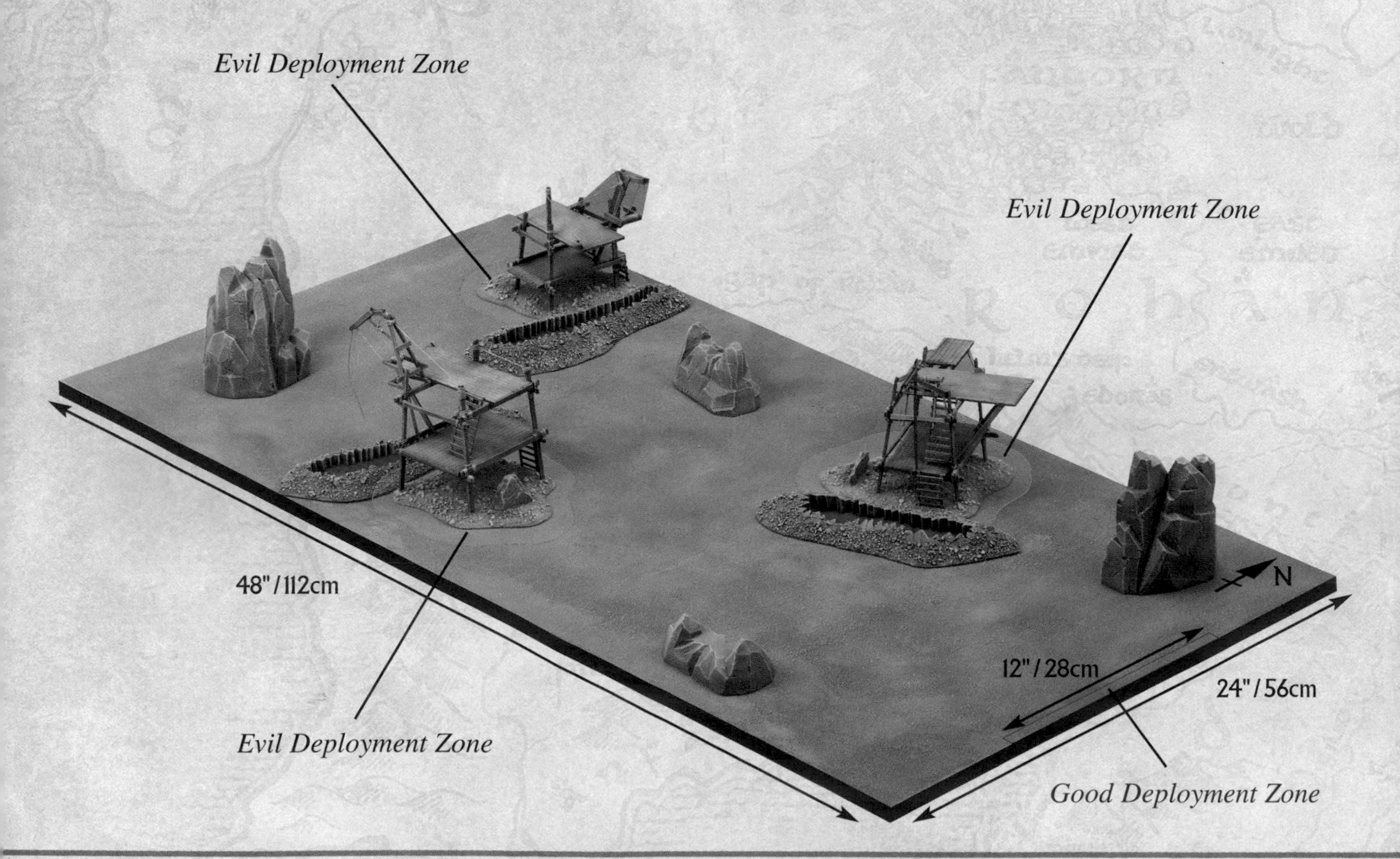

STARTING POSITIONS

The Good models are placed in contact with the western board edge, within 6"/14cm of the centre (representing the break in the outer wall). The Evil player divides his force into three equal groups. Starting with the Evil player, both players then take it in turn to place a group within 3"/8cm of any of the constructions until all the Evil models are deployed.

OBJECTIVES

Driven to a great and terrible rage the Ents have come to Orthanc to avenge themselves on Saruman's vile treason. The Good side wins if all three of Saruman's constructions are destroyed. Should Treebeard be slain, the best result that the Good side can achieve is a draw.

The Evil side wins if they wipe out the Good side before the Good side achieves their objective.

SPECIAL RULES

Orcish Structures. In the furnaces beneath Orthanc, Saruman has bred, armed and armoured his mighty force. Dotted around the Circle of Isengard are a number of his ingenious structures that have aided him in doing this – winches, bellows and all manner of machinery hewn from the trees of Fangorn and put to Evil uses. Treebeard and the Ents must destroy all three structures to win the scenario, and each counts as a siege target with a Defence of 10 and 6 Batter Points.

Orcs of Isengard. For the purposes of this scenario the Evil side is never considered to be Broken, regardless of casualties. Also, any Evil Warrior that is slain may be able to re-enter play. At the end of each Evil Move phase, roll a D6 for each Evil model that has been removed as a casualty. On the score of a 4, 5 or 6, it is available as a reinforcement, and is moved into play from the point shown on the map. Models that do not arrive as reinforcements may not be rolled for again and should be put aside.

Merry and Pippin. Though far from the heroes of this battle, the Hobbits still have their part to play in Saruman's downfall. To represent their small influence in the attack on Orthanc, the Good player may make a special shooting attack with Treebeard each turn. Regardless of how far Treebeard has moved, or even if he is in combat, Merry and Pippin can each throw a stone. These stones hit on a 3+, have a Strength of 1 and a Range of 8"/20cm. Obviously these attacks cannot target something in combat with Treebeard himself, but they can be used to shoot over his opponents at other nearby enemies. Merry and Pippin cannot be targeted themselves.

POINTS MATCH

GOOD (550 points)

Must include four models, none of which should cost less than 100 points.

EVIL (575 points)

May include two Heroes. Only one model in the force may cost more than 60 points. No more than a third of the Evil force carry bows, and no Evil models may ride steeds of any type.

THE JOURNEY TO MORDOR

With the death of Boromir and the sundering of the Fellowship, Frodo and Sam alone must press on towards Mordor and the Crack of Doom. The road before them is arduous and long, but Frodo and Sam are unswerving in their resolve and joined together by an unbreakable bond of friendship.

Along their way, they encounter the creature Gollum. This meeting is of great fortune and, thanks to Gollum's own hunger for the Ring, Frodo and Sam force him to show them the way to Mordor. Only with Gollum's grudging guidance can they hope to reach their destination, and, despite the dangers, they keep company with him.

From the rocky slopes of Emyn Muil, across the treacherous paths of the Dead Marshes and into the wilderness realm of Ithilien the three must travel. To reach their goal, they must battle Spectres and Orcs, outwit Haradrim warriors, escape a Mûmak, persuade Faramir to their cause and overcome a Nazgûl. The fate of Middle-earth lies in the hands of two Hobbits and their strange companion, and though their task seems insurmountable, hope remains that they might yet succeed.

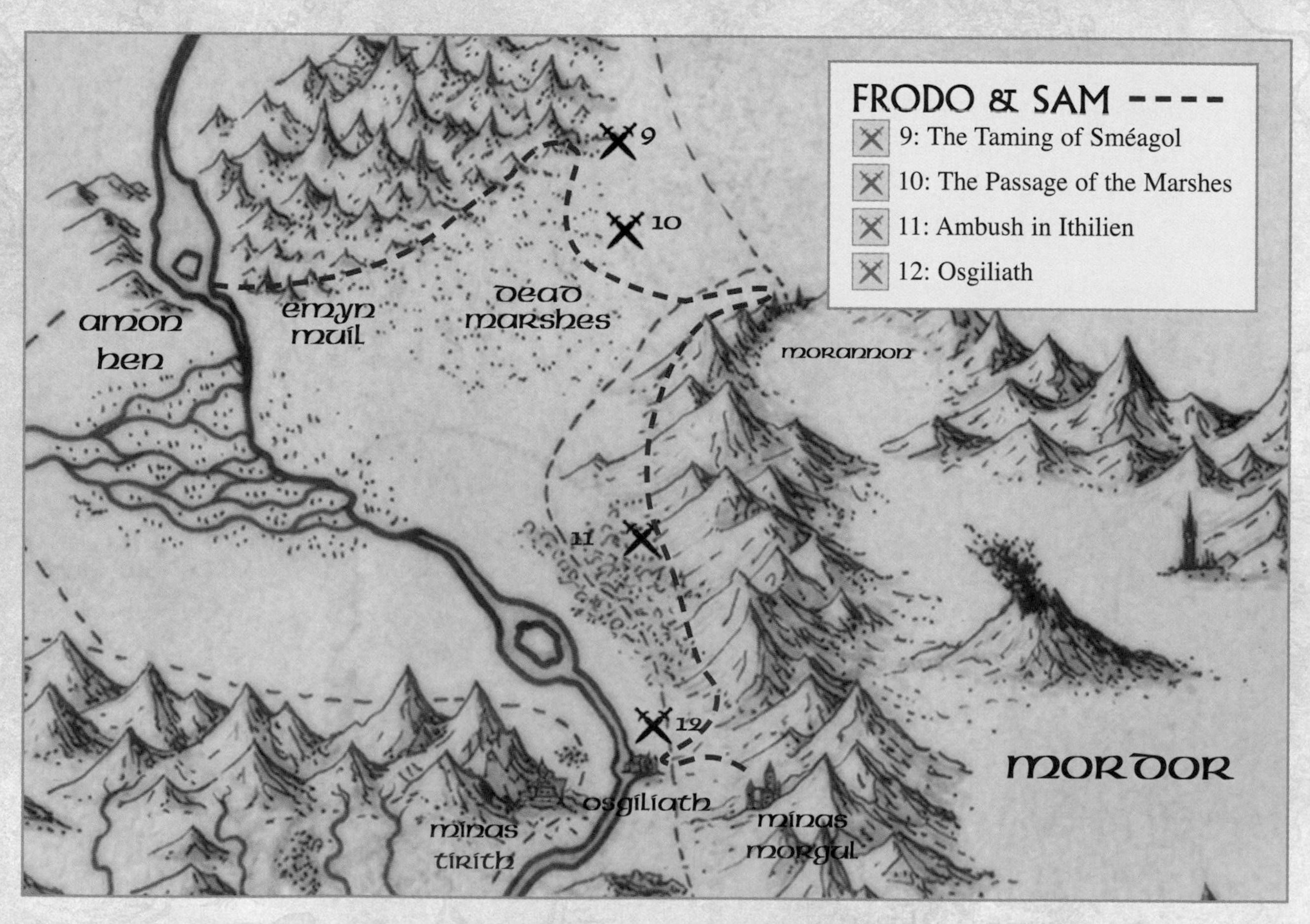

FRODO

Frodo Baggins is the bearer of the Ring of Power – he must destroy the Ring in Mordor before he falls under its sway himself. He appears in The Taming of Sméagol (scenario 9), The Passage of the Marshes (scenario 10) and Ambush at Ithilien (scenario 11).

FRODO

Hair: Chaos Black, Codex Grey

Trousers: Scorched Brown/Chaos Black, Codex Grey

Jacket: Dark Flesh, Dark Flesh/Bleached Bone

Skin: Tanned Flesh, Dwarf Flesh, Elf Flesh

Waistcoat: Scorched Brown, Bleached Bone

STING

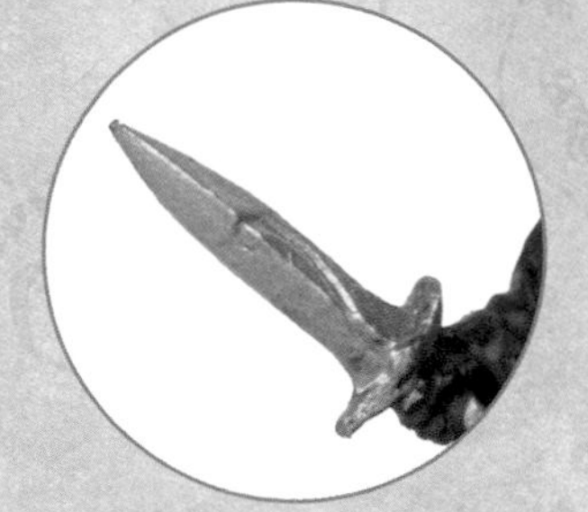

Basecoat Sting with Boltgun Metal.

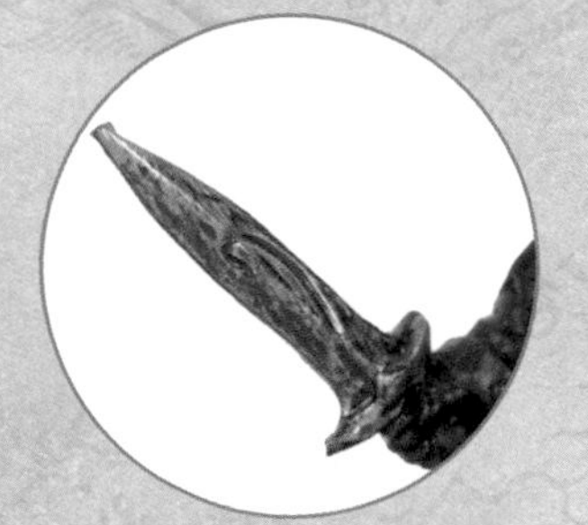

Apply a Black Ink wash.

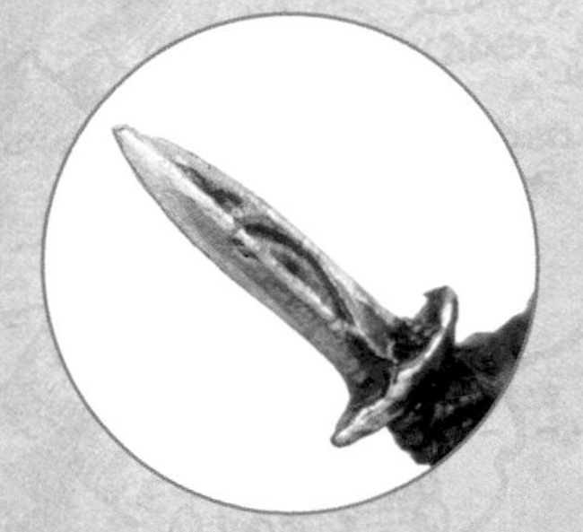

Paint a fine highlight of Mithril Silver on the edge of the blade.

SAM

Sam Gamgee is Frodo's servant and support on the journey to Mordor. Sam is always at Frodo's side, and appears in The Taming of Sméagol (scenario 9), The Passage of the Marshes (scenario 10) and Ambush in Ithilien (scenario 11).

SAM

Backpack: Codex Grey, Fortress Grey

Hair: Bestial Brown, Snakebite Leather

Jacket: Chaos Black/Codex Grey, Codex Grey

Metal: Boltgun Metal, Chainmail, Mithril Silver

Skin: Tanned Flesh, Dwarf Flesh, Elf Flesh

Trousers: Dark Angels Green, Goblin Green

Waistcoat: Bleached Bone, Skull White

ELVEN CLOAK

Basecoat with a mix of Bleached Bone and Chaos Black.

Add Bleached Bone to the basecoat and apply as a highlight.

Finish the highlight by adding more Bleached Bone to the mix.

GOLLUM

Gollum lost the Ring to Bilbo Baggins, Frodo's uncle, and he is eager to recover his precious by whatever means he can. Gollum appears in The Taming of Sméagol (scenario 9) and The Passage through the Marshes (scenario 10).

GOLLUM

- **Hair:** Codex Grey, Fortress Grey
- **Loincloth:** Scorched Brown, Bestial Brown
- **Fish:** Space Wolves Grey, Skull White

ROCKS

Start with a basecoat mix of Chaos Black and Codex Grey.

Drybrush the rocks with Codex Grey.

Finish off with a lighter drybrush of Fortress Grey.

SKIN

Paint a basecoat of Dark Flesh.

Add Fortress Grey to Dark Flesh and highlight.

Add more Fortress Grey to the highlight mix.

Add Skull White to the mix and apply the finest highlights.

EYES

Paint the eyes Skull White.

Use a small amount of Chaos Black to dot in the pupil.

ALTERNATIVE MODELS

Due to the large amount of models available, many of the major characters have alternative models, such as the two Gollums shown at the top of this page, and you're completely free to use whichever one you choose. After all, it's always more fun to use your favourite models.

MORGUL STALKERS

The Morgul Stalkers seek out the Hobbits in the wilderness. They are silent killers from Minas Morgul, the tower of the Witch-king, and are used in The Passage of the Marshes (scenario 10) and Osgiliath (scenario 12).

MORGUL STALKERS

Blades: Boltgun Metal, Chainmail, Black Ink, Mithril Silver

Cloak: Chaos Black, Codex Grey

Hair: Graveyard Earth, Snakebite Leather

Leather: Scorched Brown, Bestial Brown

Skin: Catachan Green, Fortress Grey

SPECTRES

The Spectres are the spirits of Men, Elves and Orcs, slain long ago at the Battle of Dagorlad. As the Morgul Stalkers close in, they rise to lure Frodo and Sam into danger in The Passage of the Marshes (scenario 10).

PAINTING ARMOUR

Spectres were once Elves, Men or Orcs and the armour they wear reflects this. For more information on painting the different styles of metal see the relevant race's painting guides.

Start with a base colour of Shadow Grey.

Next, paint a layer of Fortress Grey to the raised areas.

To finish, apply a Green Ink wash.

EMYN MUIL

Lost in the razor sharp crags of Emyn Muil, Frodo and Sam encounter Gollum for the first time, and, after a struggle, force him to lead them out of the labyrinthine hills. To recreate this rocky terrain, build piles of rocks of various sizes and place them on the grey board – we show how here.

MATERIALS

Polystyrene foam
Ready-mix filler
Gravel
Stones
Sand
PVA glue
Textured paint

2. Apply a little filler to the rocks followed by gravel and stones.

1. Cut a rock shape from polystyrene foam, with smaller pieces glued on top, and sculpted into crag shapes.

3. Apply textured paint before finishing your rocks to match the crags on page 12.

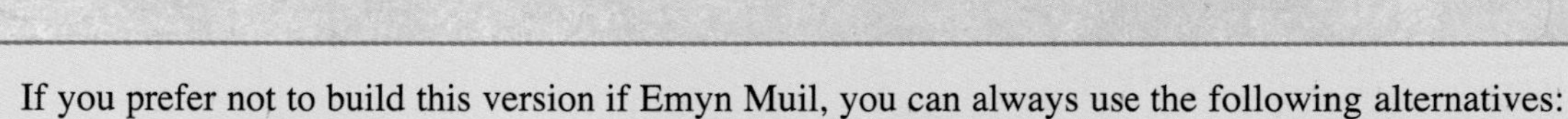

If you prefer not to build this version if Emyn Muil, you can always use the following alternatives:

Use the rocky outcrops from The Fellowship of The Ring.

Rock piles can be made from stones taken from the garden.

Glue them to a base then paint them to match the rest of your scenery.

SCENARIO 9

THE TAMING OF SMÉAGOL

Frodo and Sam have made slow progress since they split from the Fellowship. Having left their boat behind, the two Hobbits set off on their own towards Mordor and the rocky landscape of the Emyn Muil. On the third evening after setting out, Frodo and Sam once again felt the presence of the vile slinker, Gollum, creeping after them, to rescue "the precious" with his cruel, strangling hands.

FORCES

Good

Frodo Baggins with Sting, mithril coat and Elven cloak
Sam Gamgee with Elven cloak

EVIL

Sméagol

LAYOUT

This scenario is played on a board 24"/56cm x 24"/56cm. The board represents a bleak, stony gully with rocky outcrops and the occasional, withered tree. The east edge of the board represents a stone rock-face – one wall of the gully. There should also be two large rocky outcrops, three or four small rocky outcrops placed and two rocky fissures (see map).

STARTING POSITIONS

The Good player deploys Frodo and Sam within 3"/8cm of the centre of the board, behind one of the rocky outcrops as shown. The Evil player then places Gollum anywhere touching the eastern board edge.

OBJECTIVES

The Good side wins if Frodo and Sam can subdue Gollum and survive the scenario. Gollum thirsts solely for the One Ring, and the Evil player wins if Gollum can slay the Ringbearer (at which point he steals the ring and escapes). If Sam is slain, but Frodo survives, the game is a draw.

> *"Where are they with my Precious? Curse them! We hates them."*
>
> *Gollum, The Two Towers*

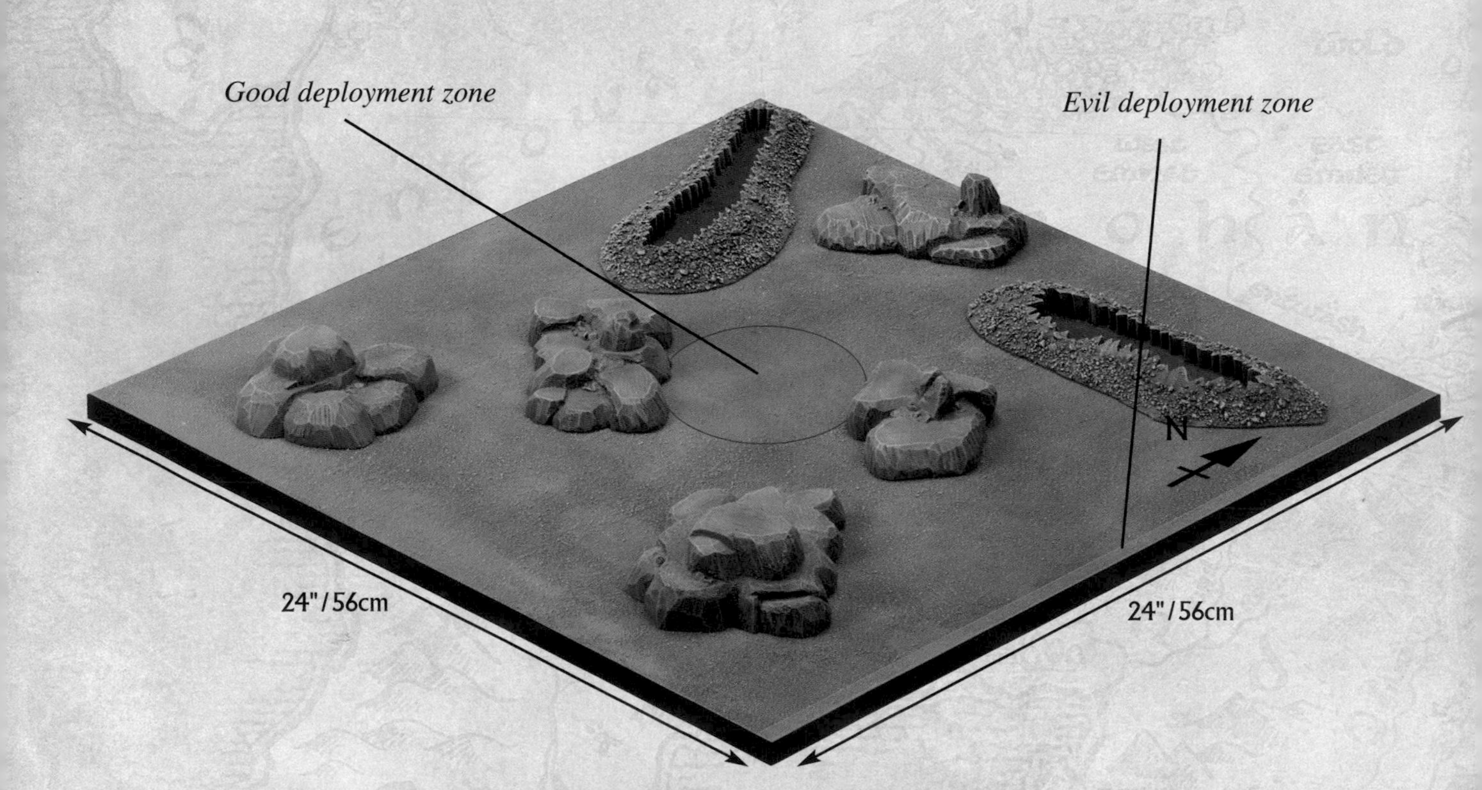

SPECIAL RULES

Gollum. Sméagol is completely lost at the moment, and Gollum has complete control. The two Hobbits are fighting for their survival, and may strike blows against Gollum as normal.

Subduing Gollum. Though Frodo and Sam are repulsed by the creature Gollum, they do not wish to kill him. In this scenario Frodo and Sam wound Gollum as normal, however if played as part of a campaign, these wounds are automatically recovered after the game. Instead of being slain, when he loses his last wound, Gollum is considered subdued. Gollum has no such qualms, however, and Frodo and Sam's wounds are treated normally.

Sting. Gollum has seen Sting before and rightly fears its power. Any time Gollum loses a fight against Frodo, he must pass a Courage test or he will surrender to the Hobbits and counts as subdued.

Scenario Note. If you want to play this scenario to match the film, add the following special rule (and lie the Hobbits down at the start of the game, to show they are asleep):

Frodo and Sam are sleeping fitfully, completely unaware of Gollum sneaking up on them. As Gollum approaches there is a chance that the loose stones and scree will be disturbed enough to create a sound, waking the Hobbits. The Hobbits start the gaming lying down, and may not act until they are woken. Should Gollum attack a sleeping Hobbit, he will automatically win the fight, but the Hobbits will be woken immediately after that Fight phase.

Before moving Gollum, the controlling player must roll a D6 (doubling the result if playing in cm). If the score is higher than the distance in inches/centimetres from Gollum to the Hobbits or a 6, then the Hobbits have been woken and may act normally from this point onwards. Gollum may use Might to influence this roll.

POINTS MATCH

GOOD (150 points)

Must include two Good Heroes, neither of which may have more than 2 Wounds.

EVIL (150 points)

Must include a single Evil Hero, with a points value roughly equal to the Good side.

RINGWRAITH ON FELL BEAST

The Ringwraith on Fell Beast hunts the Ringbearer at Sauron's command. A terrifying, magical opponent mounted on a flying beast, the Ringwraith appears in The Passage of the Marshes (scenario 10).

RINGWRAITH

Cloak: Chaos Black, Chaos Black/Codex Grey, Codex Grey

Metal: Tin Bitz, Boltgun Metal, Chainmail

PINNING

Pinning helps to strengthen joins for larger models such as this. We recommend that you use a pin vice to join the three parts of the body together. Once this is done, you can pin the legs in place.

WINGS

Drybrush Codex Grey onto the creature's skin.

Then drybrush Graveyard Earth on top.

Finally, apply a drybrush of Kommando Khaki.

BELLY

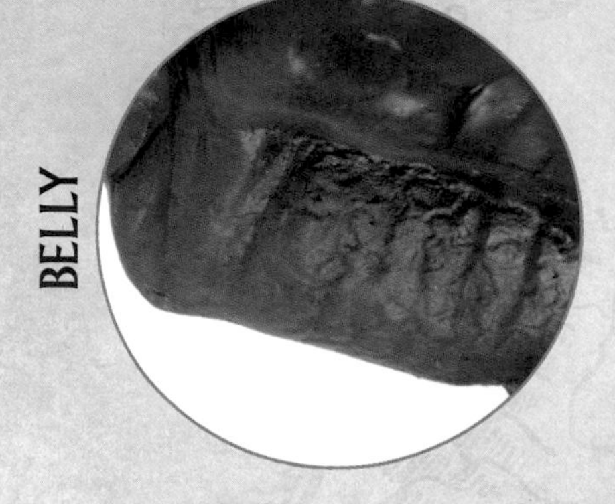

Stipple on a mix of Chaos Black and Codex Grey.

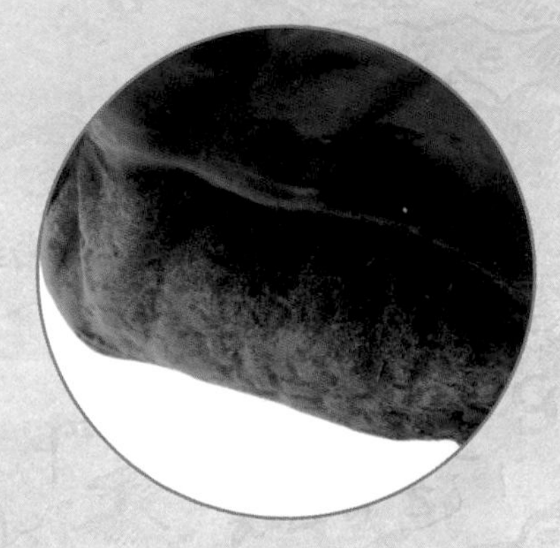

Then stipple on a Codex Grey and Dwarf Flesh mix.

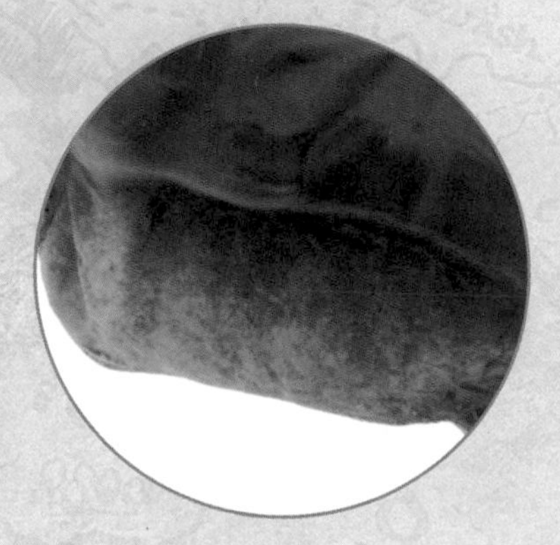

Finally, stipple on a mix of Fortress Grey and Elf Flesh.

SKIN

To paint the skin, drybrush the following colours.

- Codex Grey,
- Fortress Grey,
- Rotting Flesh

TEETH

The teeth have been picked out with Bleached Bone.

THE FELL BEAST'S BASE

Modelled onto the tail of the Fell Beast is a piece of ruined wall from Osgiliath, which adds extra support to the model on the base. Once you've applied a layer of sand, paint the base and the stone wall to match your Osgiliath ruins on page 58.

FRODO

As he perfectly captures the moment from the film, this particular Frodo is ideal for using in the film version of the Osgiliath scenario on page 62.

THE DEAD MARSHES

Gollum leads Frodo and Sam through the Dead Marshes, a treacherous quagmire menaced by Spectres and Morgul Stalkers. Building a marshland allows you to make any amount of enclosed terrain pieces.

1. Cut a base and glue a layer of foamboard onto the surface.

2. Remove the top layer of card and use a sculpting tool to gouge furrows into the foam.

ALTERNATIVE OPTION

If you'd prefer not to make specific pieces of marshland for this scenario, use coloured card cut into oval shapes instead.

MATERIALS

Wooden basing material
5mm thick foamboard
Gravel
Sand
PVA glue

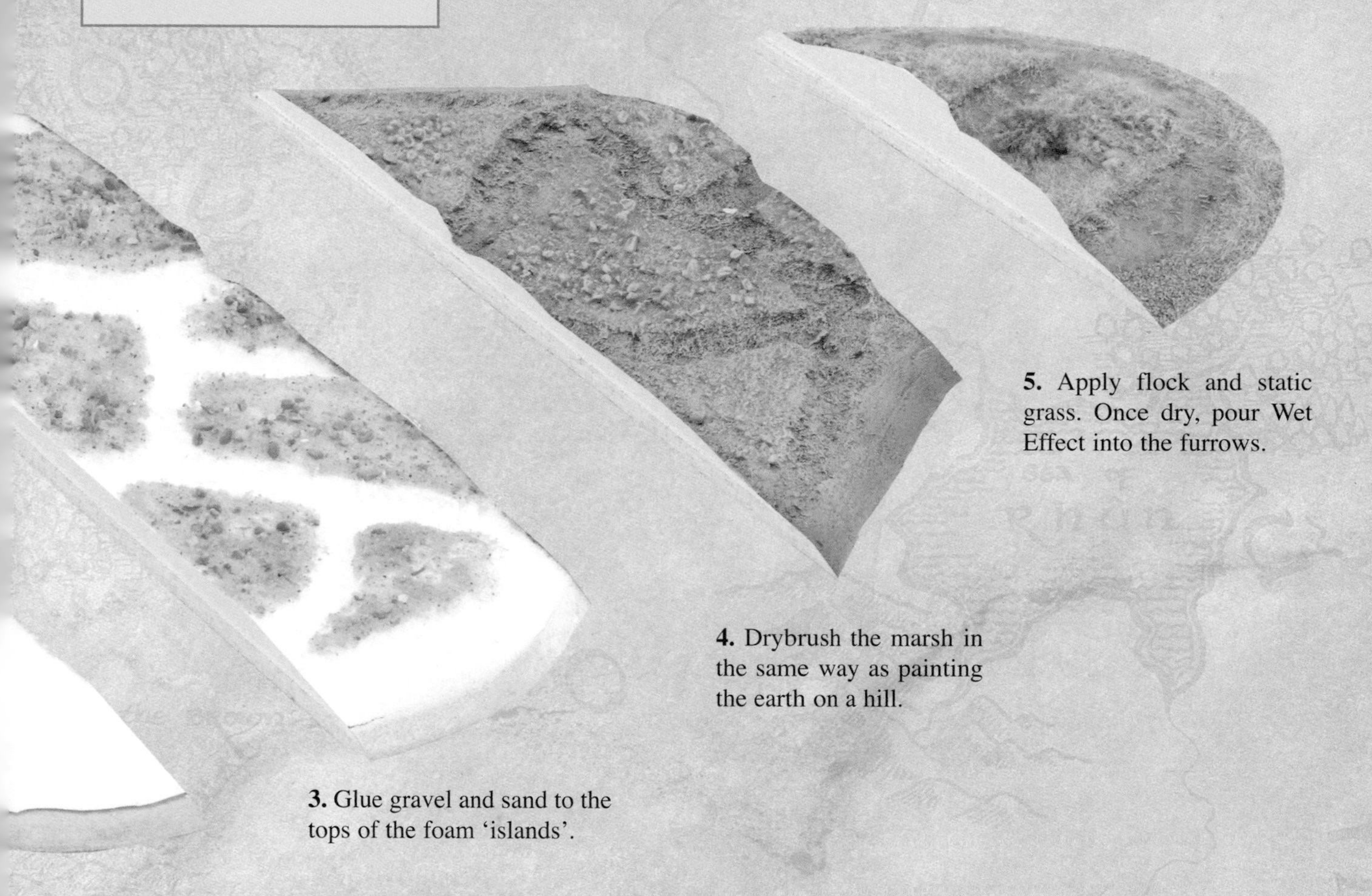

5. Apply flock and static grass. Once dry, pour Wet Effect into the furrows.

4. Drybrush the marsh in the same way as painting the earth on a hill.

3. Glue gravel and sand to the tops of the foam 'islands'.

HOW TO USE WET EFFECT

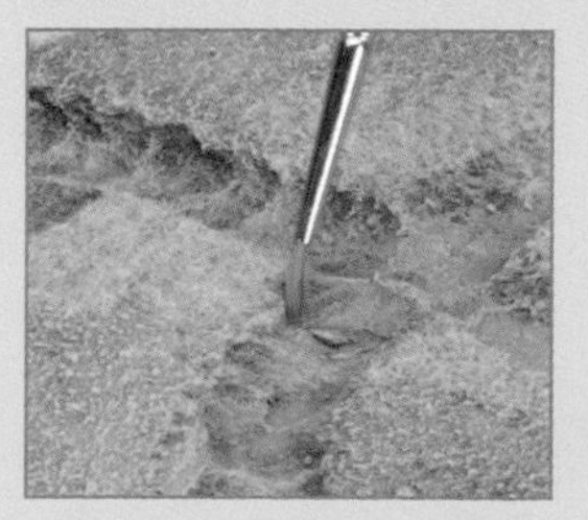

1. Use a clean brush to clear off any excess dust or flock.

2. Pour Wet Effect into the furrows, about 2-3mm deep.

3. Use a clean brush to push the Wet Effect into the corners of the furrows.

4. Leave to dry overnight on a level surface.

SCENARIO 10

THE PASSAGE OF THE MARSHES

Frodo and Sam leave behind the rough and dangerous country of the Emyn Muil as they continue onwards to Mordor. Choosing to avoid the barren plain of Dagorlad, where the highways of Orcs run, Gollum leads the Hobbits into the Dead Marshes. These desolate fens are forever wreathed in clammy fog that is filled with the beguiling lights of the dead spectres that haunt this forsaken region. As Gollum leads them deeper and deeper into the marshes, it soon becomes clear that they are not alone…

PARTICIPANTS

GOOD

Frodo with Sting, mithril coat and Elven cloak
Sam with Elven cloak
Sméagol

EVIL

Ringwraith (on Fell Beast)
3 Spectres
6 Morgul Stalkers

LAYOUT

The scenario is played on a board 36"/84cm by 36"/84cm and takes place in the Dead Marshes. The entire board is covered in boggy terrain, patches of scrub and low bushes. Place one marsh, roughly 6"/14cm in diameter, in the centre of the board and three others around it, towards the corners of the board, leaving gaps big enough for models to pass through (see map).

STARTING POSITIONS

Frodo, Sam and Gollum start in base contact with the centre of the western board edge. Place a Spectre in the centre of three of the deep marshes, then place two Morgul Stalkers in base contact with the centre of the eastern, southern and northern board edges. The Ringwraith on Fell Beast starts in base contact with the eastern board edge. No Evil model may start the game closer than 12"/28cm to any Good model.

"The tricksy lights. Candles of corpses, yes, yes."

Gollum, The Two Towers.

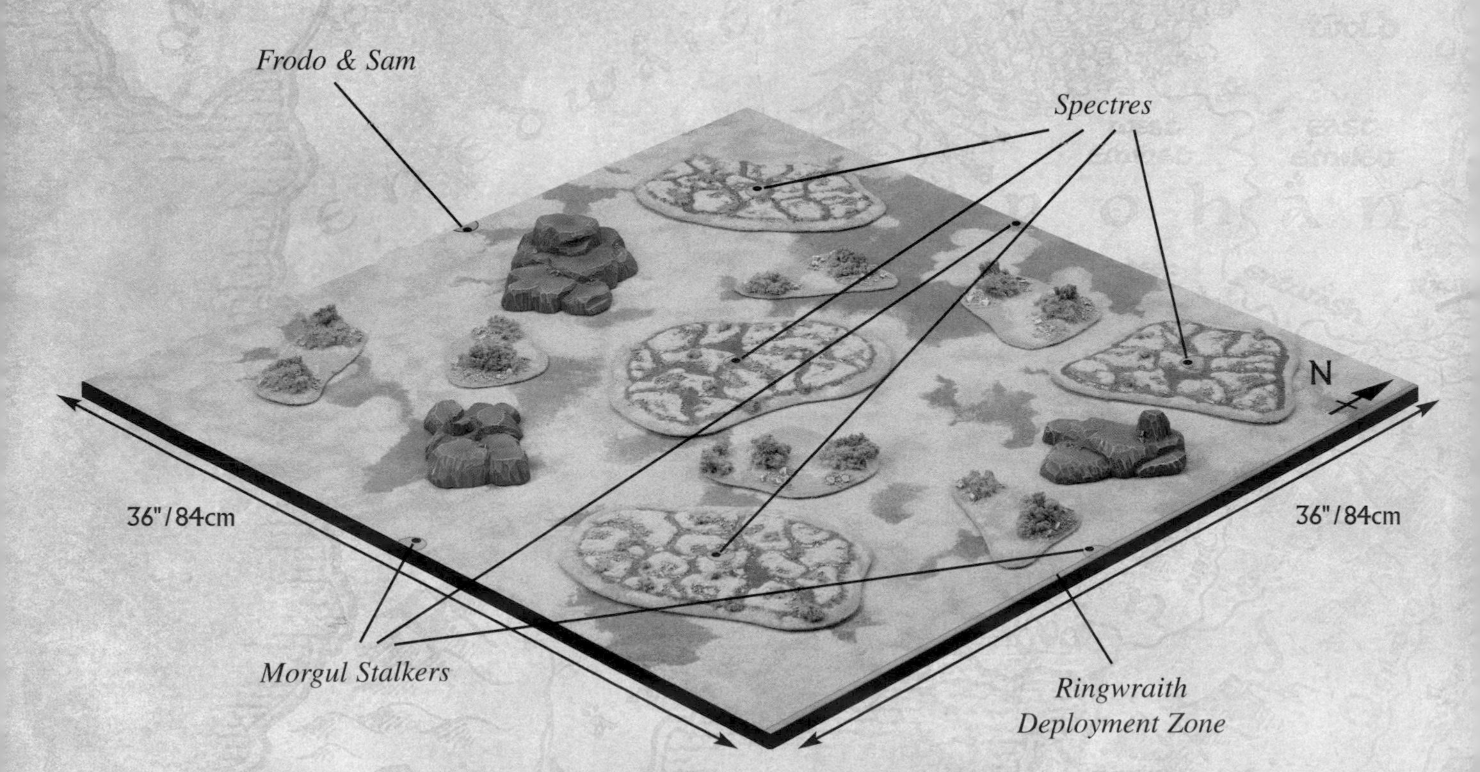

OBJECTIVES

Frodo and Sam must pass through the Dead Marshes to continue their journey to Mordor and destroy the Ring. The Good player wins if Frodo is able to move off the eastern board edge. The Evil player wins if Frodo dies.

SPECIAL RULES

I will serve the master of the Precious. In this scenario, Sméagol is under the control of the Good player.

The Dead Marshes. The pools of deep marsh are treacherous and many a foolhardy traveller has been lured to his death within their clammy embrace. Models not wearing armour count the marshes as difficult terrain, but models wearing armour (with the exception of Spectres) that enter a deep marsh must roll on the Swimming chart in the main rules manual.

Hunt the Ringbearer. The Morgul Stalkers and Spectres follow the rules for sentries given in the main rules manual, with the exception that if a sentry becomes aware of the Hobbits, it is only that model that may move, shoot and fight as normal from then on.

Wraiths with wings! The Ringwraith follows the rules for sentries given in the main rules manual until one of the Morgul Stalkers becomes aware of the Hobbits. During any turn where a Morgul Stalker is aware of the Hobbits, the Ringwraith may act as normal for the duration of that turn. If no Stalkers are aware of the Hobbits, then the Ringwraith may not act, even if any Good models are within 4"/10cm of the Ringwraith at the end of their move. The Ringwraith has been searching for the Ringbearer for many moons now, and therefore starts the game with no Might or Fate and 10 Will points.

POINTS MATCH

Good (150 points)

Must include three Heroes. No Hero may be mounted on a steed.

Evil (275 points)

Must include one Hero on a steed to represent the Ringwraith on Fell Beast. May not include any other mounted models or models with bows of any kind.

MÛMAK

The Mûmak is a vast creature from the lands to the south of Middle-earth. It tramples its enemies underfoot, carries Haradrim warriors into battle on its back and makes its first appearance at the Ambush in Ithilien (scenario 11).

MÛMAK

Cloth: Scab Red, Tanned Flesh

Wood: Scorched Brown, Bestial Brown

Rope: Graveyard Earth, Bleached Bone

ASSEMBLY INSTRUCTIONS

The Mûmak comes with a set of instructions to help you assemble the model. Some people prefer to keep the howdah, the Mûmak and the base separate from each other to make painting easier, and gluing the whole kit together at the end.

SKIN

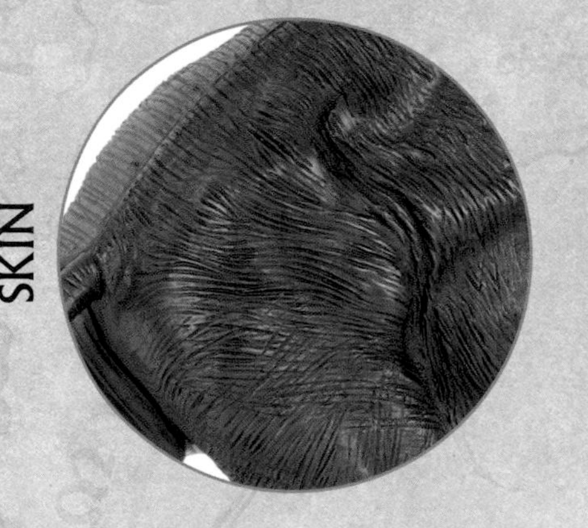

Start by drybrushing with a mix of Chaos Black and Codex Grey.

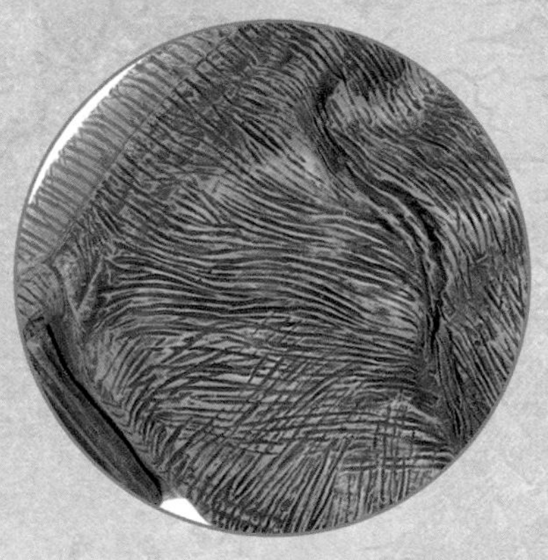

Then drybrush the skin Codex Grey.

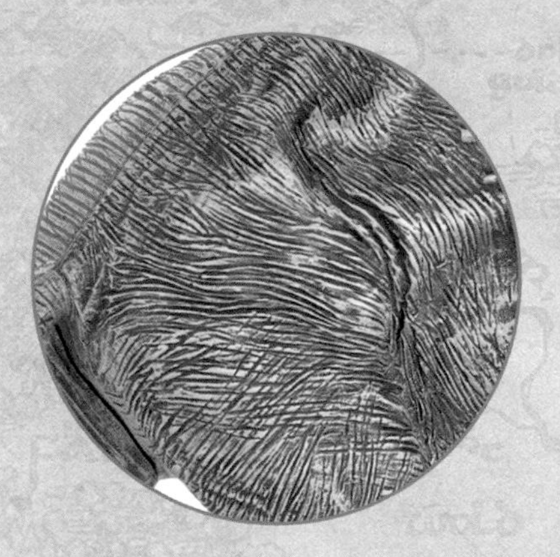

Apply a final drybrush mix of Codex Grey and Bleached Bone.

TUSKS

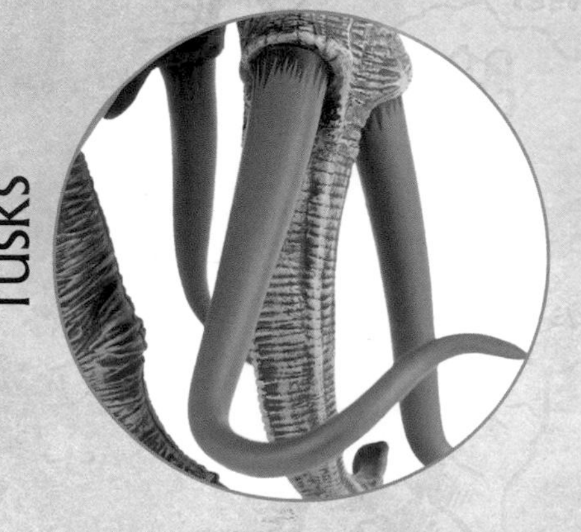

Over a basecoat of Scorched Brown, layer Bestial Brown onto the tusks.

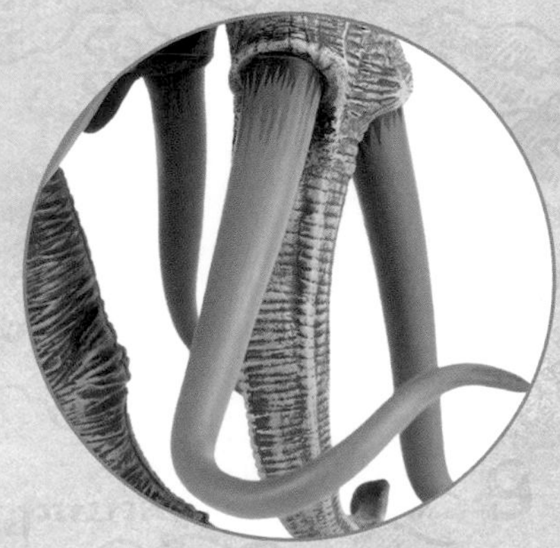

Then layer on stripes of Snakebite Leather.

Finally paint on stripes of Bleached Bone.

THE MÛMAK'S BASE

The model's base is covered in lots of detail but is quite straightforward to paint.

The Rohirrim and their horses are painted using the Rohan colour palette on page 16.

For more information on painting Orcs see the painting guide on page 9.

Paint the earth to match the rest of the bases in your collection.

HARADRIM

Haradrim are one of the races of evil Men who are allied to Sauron's forces. These warriors from the south use poisoned arrows and ride to war on the back of a Mûmak in the Ambush in Ithilien (scenario 11).

HARADRIM

Flesh: Dwarf Flesh mixed with Bronzed Flesh

Gems: Hawk Turquoise, Skull White

Cloth: Liche Purple or Warlock Purple or Red Gore

Metal: Boltgun Metal, Black Ink, Chainmail

HARADRIM ARMOUR

Basecoat the armour Shining Gold.

Then apply a Brown Ink wash.

Highlight with a mix of Shining Gold and Mithril Silver.

PAINTING

RANGERS OF GONDOR

Rangers of Gondor are one of the many bands of warriors who protect the wilderness around Osgiliath from the enemies of Gondor. They are keen-eyed bowmen who ambush their foes rather than attack them head on, such as at the Ambush in Ithilien (scenario 11) and Osgiliath (scenario 12).

RANGERS

- **Bows:** Scorched Brown, Dark Flesh
- **Cloak:** Catachan Green, Camo Green
- **Cloth:** Dark Angels Green, Catachan Green or Scorched Brown, Bestial Brown or Scorched Brown/Scab Red, Scab Red
- **Leather:** Scorched Brown, Bestial Brown
- **Skin:** Tanned Flesh, Dwarf Flesh

WEATHERED CLOAKS

Drybrush the edge of the cloak Scorched Brown.

Finish off the edges with a drybrush of Graveyard Earth.

RANGER HEROES

Characters such as Faramir, Madril and Damrod are painted in the same way as the troops they command. As their heads are visible they are the sort of models that reward painting extra detail.

Faramir

Madril

Damrod

OSGILIATH VETERANS

The Osgiliath Veterans defend their ruined city from the forces of Mordor. They are heavily armoured and skilful warriors, who fight side by side with the Rangers of Gondor in Osgiliath (scenario 12).

VETERANS

- **Cloaks:** Scorched Brown, Graveyard Earth
- **Skin:** Bestial Brown, Dwarf Flesh
- **Tunics:** Chaos Black, Codex Grey
- **Wood:** Chaos Black, Codex Grey

DRYBRUSHING ARMOUR

We've made a feature of the armour on these troops, applying extra layers of paint to make them look very distinct. However, if you prefer you can apply the colours using drybrushing, which can also look very effective.

ARMOUR

Start by basecoating the armour Boltgun Metal.

Shade the armour with watered-down Chaos Black.

Apply highlights of Chainmail.

Then final highlights of Mithril Silver.

EXTRA DETAILS

The great thing about the Osgiliath Veterans is the sheer amount of detail the miniatures possess. With their combination of patchwork cloaks, bedrolls, beaten armour and assorted equipment, you can take the time to make them look like the battered veterans they are.

OSGILIATH RUINS

Osgiliath has been devastated by countless attacks from the forces of Mordor and the once-proud city is now nothing more than a ruin. To represent Osgiliath on the table top, start with a few ruined buildings on a grey board. No ruin should be the same as another, so that gives you lots of freedom to make models any way you want. To help get you started, here's how to make one particular ruin, that you can adapt to make different shaped buildings.

MATERIALS

- Wooden basing material
- 5mm thick foamboard
- Balsa wood
- Thin card
- PVA glue
- Textured paint

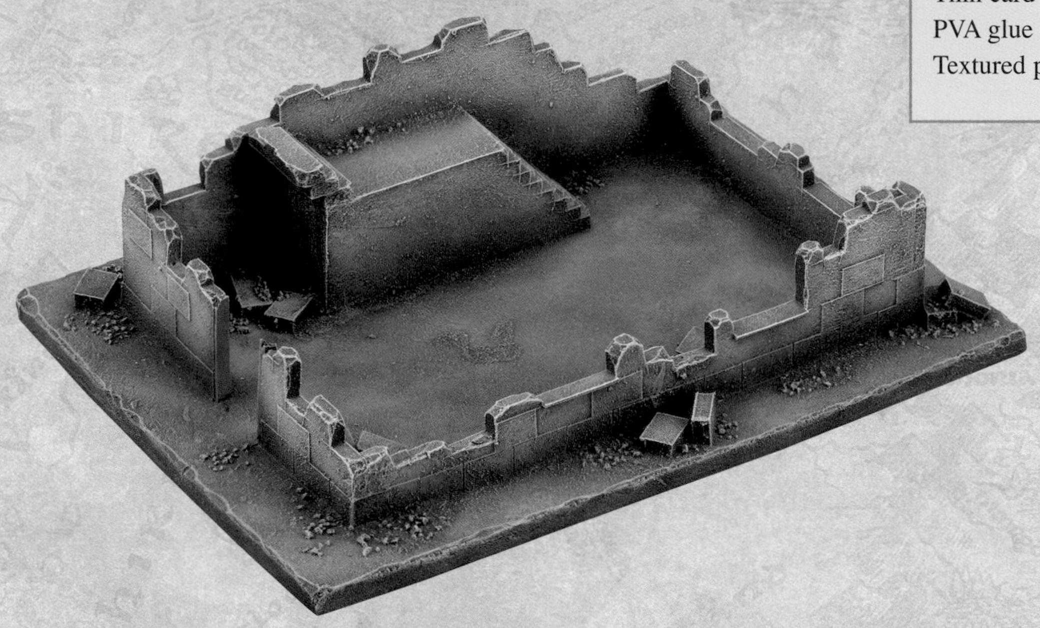

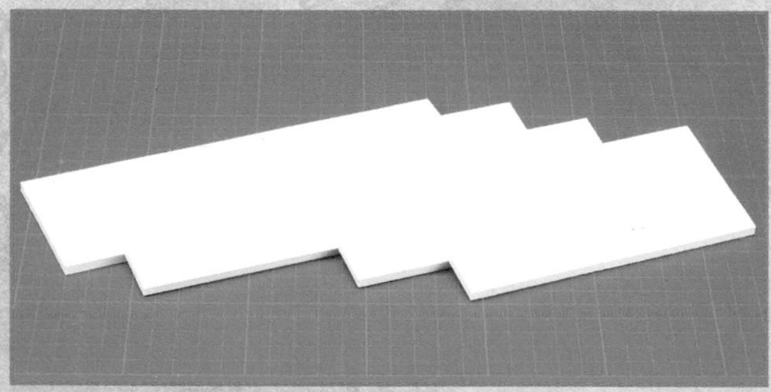

1. Start by cutting 70mm tall walls from foamboard – two 140mm wide, two 200mm.

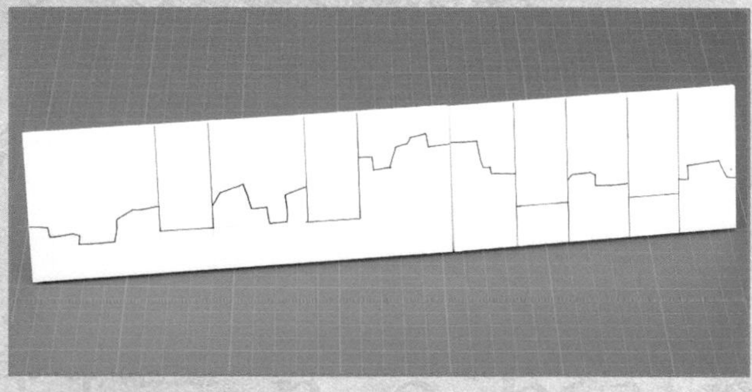

2. Draw the ruined walls with a pencil, making sure the ends follow on from each other. Make sure you mark out space for a door on one wall.

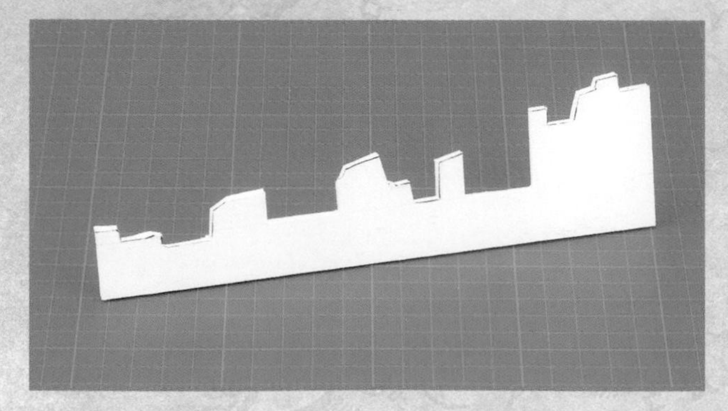

3. Use a craft knife to cut along the outline, leaving the door uncut until you've glued the walls to the base.

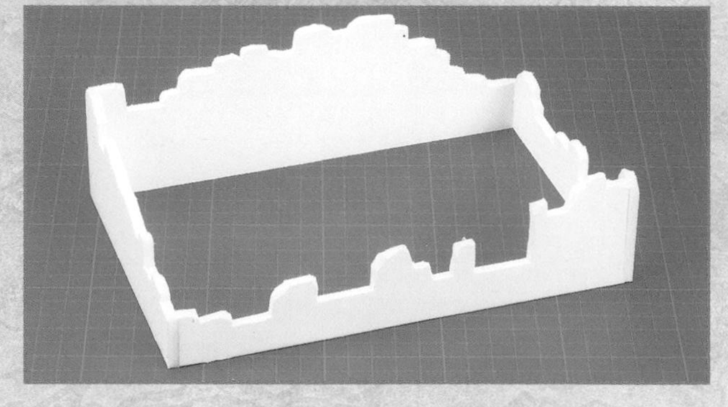

4. Next, glue the walls together. Use pins to hold the corners together until the glue sets.

5. Cut a base for the building, with a layer of foamboard glued on top. Glue the building to the base and cut out the doorway.

6. Then cut ledges from thin card to fit the windows. To give a brick pattern cut 10x15mm pieces of card and glue these to the walls.

7. Add strips of balsa into the doorway to represent doorposts.

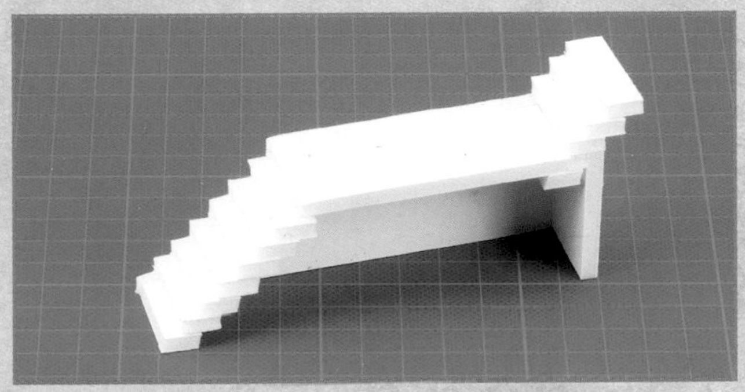

8. Build a 30mm wide stairway from foamcard, which should be no higher than the tallest wall on your ruin.

9. Glue the stairway to one of the inner walls of your building, and paint as detailed below.

You may wish to add extra rubble. This is done by gluing offcuts of foamcard to the building before you paint it.

PAINTING

1. Start by drybrushing the ruins Dark Flesh.

2. Drybrush on a mix of Graveyard Earth and Codex Grey.

3. Then apply a drybrush of Fortress Grey.

4. Finish off with a drybrush of Skull White.

SCENARIO 11

AMBUSH IN ITHILIEN

Quite by chance Frodo and Sam have fallen into the hands of the Rangers of Ithilien. Led by Faramir, Boromir's brother, these brave warriors have been stalking the wilds, laying ambush to Sauron's forces as they pass through. Having never seen a Hobbit before, and fearing some deception, the Rangers keep Frodo and Sam prisoner while they carry out their attack. As the ambush unfolds, Frodo and Sam find themselves in grave peril as the Haradrim force comes ever closer to their hiding place. Can Faramir and his Rangers keep their prisoners safe and destroy the Haradrim before they break through the ambush?

PARTICIPANTS

GOOD

Faramir with bow
Madril
Damrod
Frodo Baggins with Sting, mithril coat and Elven cloak
Sam Gamgee with Elven cloak
10 Rangers of Gondor

EVIL

1 Haradrim Chieftain with bow and spear
1 Haradrim Chieftain on horse
1 Mûmak
18 Haradrim Warriors with spear
18 Haradrim Warriors with bow
1 Haradrim Warrior with banner

LAYOUT

Set up a 48"/112cm x 48"/112cm board, with a road running between two opposite edges. Place the two large hills on the board with one against the north edge and the other against the south (see map). Place two small woods (of about three trees) within 12"/28cm of the north edge and one large wood (of about five trees) within 12"/28cm of the south edge. Lastly place as many spare trees and rocky outcrops as you have available on the board to set the scene, remembering to leave a clear space through the centre of the board to represent the road.

STARTING POSITIONS

The Hobbits are placed within 12"/28cm of the edge by which the Haradrim enter play (see map). Damrod and one other Ranger of Gondor are placed in base contact with Frodo and Sam. The rest of the Good side starts with all of its models within 12"/28cm of the north or south board edges, and in cover (Good models may be split between these two edges). This represents the Rangers lying low and waiting for the Haradrim to arrive.

All Evil models enter play in 'waves'. These waves represent the column gradually separating throughout the day's march. On the first turn, the Evil side moves both the Haradrim Chieftain on foot, and nine spear-armed Haradrim Warriors onto the board along the road.

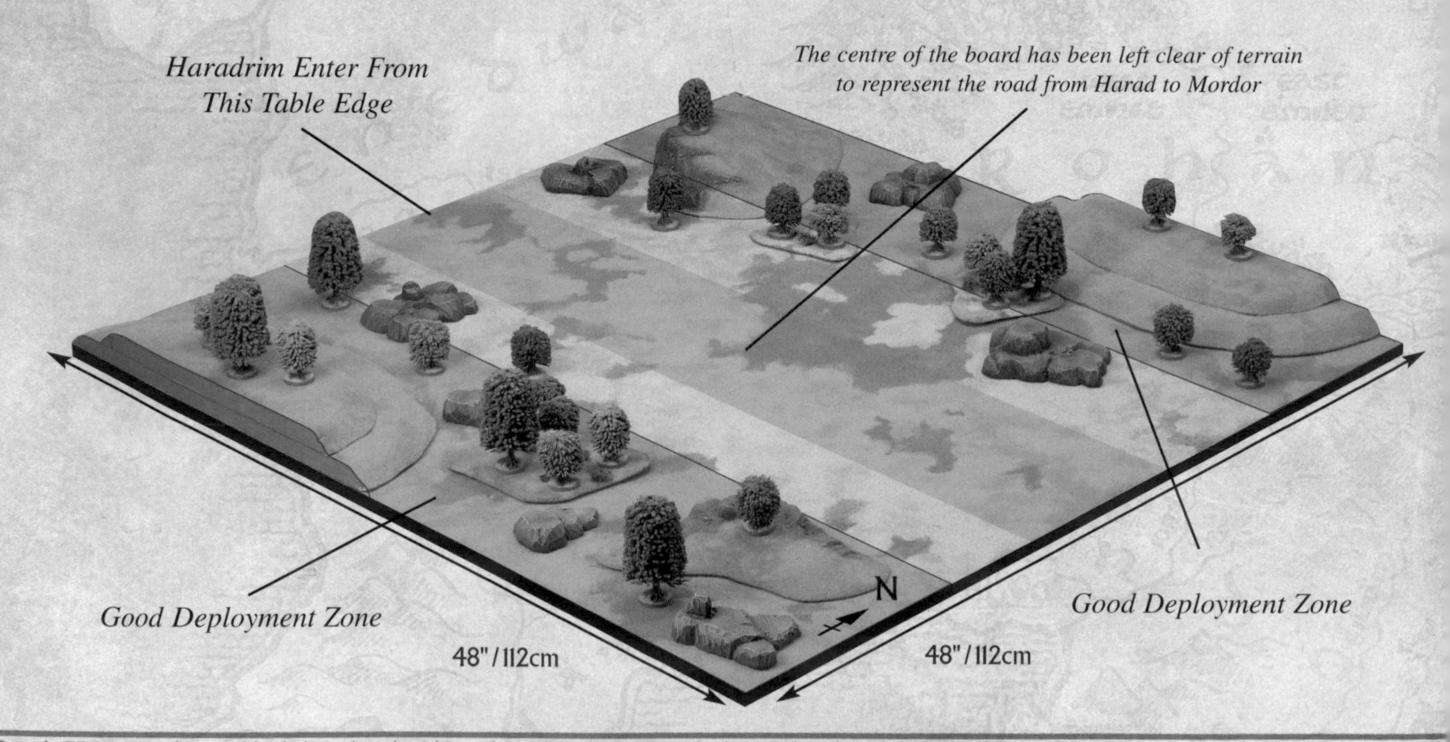

OBJECTIVES

To win the Evil player must move a third of his models off of the board edge opposite to their starting edge. Models leaving the table by any other edge count as slain.

The Good side wins if no more than a third of the total Haradrim force escapes from the board (remember, the Mûmak still counts as one!). They must do this without sustaining 50% casualties themselves. If this happens, the best result Good can achieve is a draw.

Additionally, since capturing the Hobbits, Faramir's band holds the fate of Middle-earth within their grasp. Should Frodo be slain, then the Good side automatically loses. Protecting the Hobbits is therefore imperative.

SPECIAL RULES

The Ambush. Faramir and Madril have fashioned a cunning trap for the Haradrim, with keen-eyed bowmen concealed ready to loose arrows on the Evil Men. While the Good models remain behind obstacles, and do not fire on the Haradrim, the Evil models must remain on the road. As soon as a Good model shoots his bow, or moves from cover the Haradrim will realise their peril and can act normally.

Waves. The Haradrim regiment under ambush has become separated thanks to the long day's march. To represent this, the Haradrim force is split into three waves. Once any Evil model from a wave crosses the halfway point on the board, the next wave is able to enter play in the following Evil Move phase (so it's worth remembering which group specific warriors belong to).

Each wave enters the board via the board edge (see map) along the road. Should all Evil models in a wave be slain, the next will enter play in the following Evil Move phase.

The first wave enters play in the first Evil Move phase and consists of the Haradrim Chieftain on foot and nine Haradrim Warriors with spears. The first wave of Haradrim Warriors may not leave the road until the Good player shoots at them.

The second wave consists of the Haradrim Chieftain on horseback, nine Haradrim Warriors with spear, nine Haradrim Warriors with bow and the Haradrim Warrior with banner.

The third wave consists of the Mûmak with 9 Haradrim armed with bows within the howdah.

The Southron Horde. The Haradrim convoy consists of thousands of warriors marching towards Mordor, and the warriors in this scenario are simply the vanguard. No Evil model needs to test for being Broken in this scenario.

POINTS MATCH

GOOD (375 points)

Must include at least two Good Heroes; one to represent Faramir and one to represent Frodo. No Good models may ride steeds of any kind.

EVIL (625 points)

Must include three Evil Heroes, with one placed in each wave. Each wave (see special rules) must have at least 100 points worth of models in it.

SCENARIO 12

OSGILIATH

Despite destroying the Haradrim in Ithilien, Faramir has little time to rest as Sauron's forces flood across the Anduin to drive the defenders from Osgiliath. Rushing back from their secret fastness in the wilds of Ithilien, Faramir and his Rangers race to reinforce the beleaguered garrison there. No sooner have they arrived than the next great assault begins, and he and his men are thrown into yet another desperate battle against the hosts of Morgul. The line is held by a clutch of brave veterans, who, with their captain, might yet turn back the tide of Orcs attacking the ruined city.

PARTICIPANTS

GOOD

Faramir armed with bow
Madril
Damrod
Captain of Minas Tirith with shield
6 Rangers of Gondor
3 Osgiliath Veterans with shield
3 Osgiliath Veterans with spear
3 Osgiliath Veterans with bow
1 Warrior of Minas Tirith with banner

EVIL

2 Orc Captains with shield
6 Morgul Stalkers
8 Orcs with shield
8 Orcs with spear
4 Orcs with bow
4 Orcs with two-handed weapon
2 Orcs with banner

LAYOUT

This scenario is played on a 48"/112cm x 24"/56cm table, representing a portion of the once-great city of Osgiliath. Three ruined buildings are placed on the board, as well as plenty of rubble and wreckage (see map).

STARTING POSITIONS

The Evil player deploys all of his models anywhere along the north, west or east board edge. The Good player then places his models anywhere on the board, but at least 6"/14cm from any Evil model.

OBJECTIVES

The armies of Mordor are attempting to sweep the remnants of Osgiliath's defenders away before launching their full-scale invasion. The Evil side wins if it controls more of the ruined buildings than the Good side at the end of the game. The Good side wins if it controls more of the ruined buildings than the Evil side at the end of the game. The game ends after twelve turns.

A building is controlled if one side has at least twice as many models within it than the other (or has models in the building and the enemy does not). Buildings that are not controlled in this way are 'contested' and neither side may claim it.

SPECIAL RULES

Reinforcements. Both armies are rushing extra reinforcements into the area now that battle is joined. At the end of their Movement phase, each player may attempt to bring back into play any Warriors that have been previously slain. Roll a D6 for each slain model. On a 1, 2 or 3, the model is removed and takes no further part in the game, but on the score of a 4+ it is available for reuse. Models that arrive in this fashion do so by any table edge, as chosen by the controlling player. They may not charge, but may otherwise act as normal. Both sides are flooding warriors into the area, so neither side is considered to be Broken in this scenario, regardless of casualties.

Scenario Note. If you wish to play the film version of this scenario, use the following special rules as well as those already given. Additionally, include Frodo, Sam and Gollum on the Good side, and a Ringwraith on Fell Beast on the Evil side.

Deployment & Objectives. The Good player deploys Frodo, Sam, Sméagol and Faramir 12"/28cm from the west board edge. The Nazgûl is not deployed at the start of the game, but will enter play later. Should Frodo be killed, the Evil side automatically wins. Should Frodo escape, but the Evil player controls more buildings at the end of the game, it is a draw.

Frodo and Sam. Despite their temporary capture at the hands of Faramir and his Rangers, the Hobbits have retained all their equipment and supplies. Frodo is equipped with Sting, the mithril coat and an Elven cloak. Sam has an Elven cloak.

Poor Sméagol. Gollum has taken a savage beating at the hands of the Rangers of Gondor. He is now fully resigned to betraying Frodo and stealing the Ring, but he is not so foolish as to think he can do so while Faramir and his men are watching over him. Gollum is completely under the control of the Good player for the duration of this scenario, however he may not use his Might point to perform a heroic action of any kind.

Nazgûl. One of the Nine has tracked Frodo and the Ring to Osgiliath, and seizes its chance to achieve its master's aim. In the Evil Move phase of turn three, the Nazgûl may enter play. It has 1 Might, 7 Will, 1 Fate and moves on from any point on the west board edge.

Once per game, in the Priority phase (but before any dice have been rolled) the Evil player may choose to unleash the piercing wail of the Nazgûl. This terrible cry freezes the hearts of all who hear it – accordingly all models on the Good side have their Courage reduced by 3 points for the duration of that turn.

POINTS MATCH

GOOD (375 points)

Must include at least one Hero. No Good models may ride steeds of any kind.

EVIL (375 points)

Must include at least one Hero. No Evil models may ride steeds of any kind.

THE BATTLE OF HELM'S DEEP

King Théoden has commanded his people to make for the refuge of Helm's Deep, confident the mighty fortress will never be taken so long as men defend its walls. As night falls and the flickering glow of torches is seen approaching the fortress, the true scale of the invasion becomes clear. Ten thousand Uruk-hai and Dunlendings march upon the walls, equipped with scaling ladders, grappling hooks and mighty siege engines. Thunder splits the sky and torrential rain falls as the raucous cries of Saruman's Uruk-hai signal the attack. King Théoden coordinates the defences from the Hornburg while Aragorn, Legolas and Gimli stand with the Warriors of Rohan on the ramparts as the army of Evil launches its assault. Can the walls of Helm's Deep survive this terrifying attack or will the armies of Saruman destroy the last hope of the Free People?

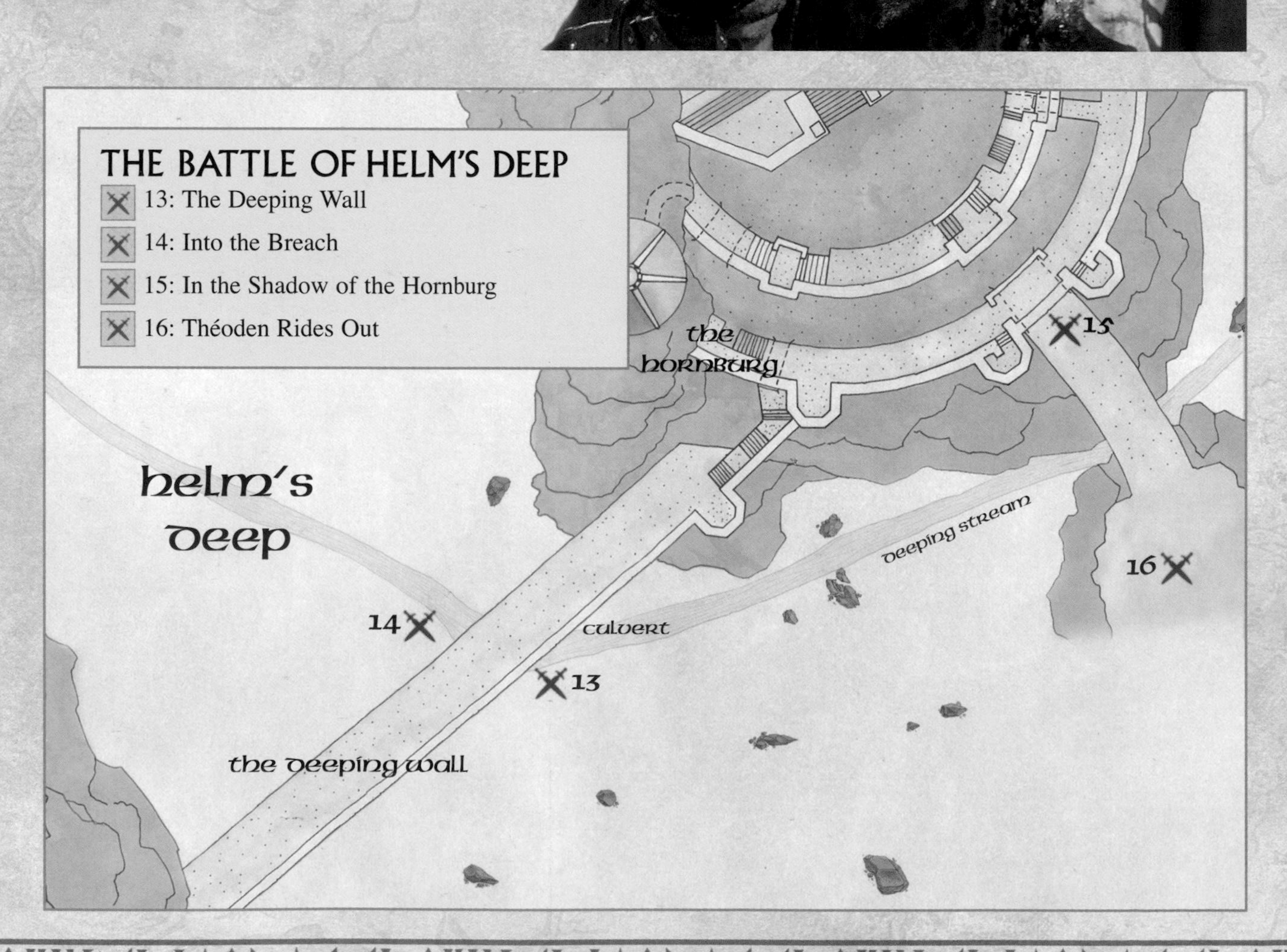

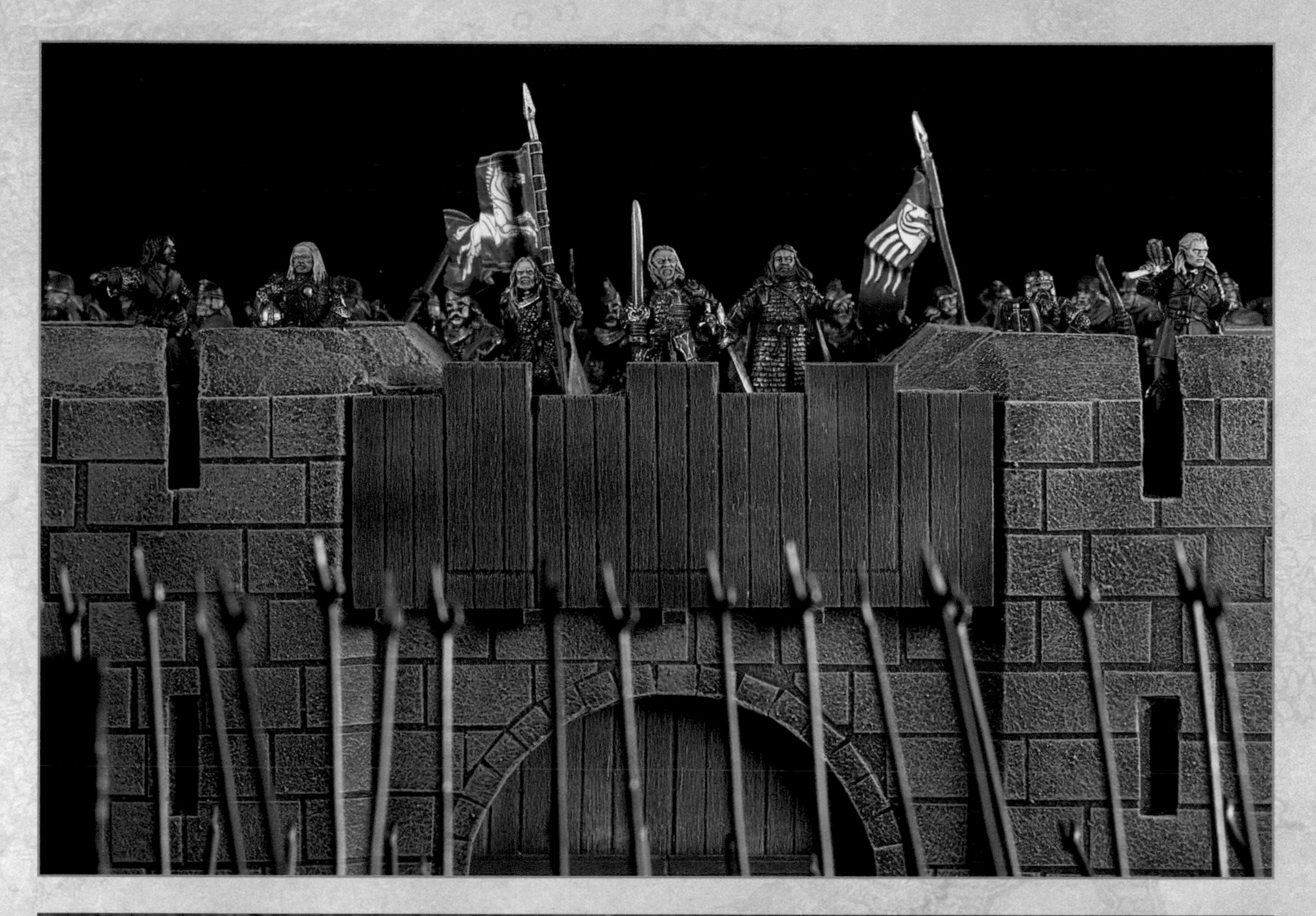

URUK-HAI WARRIORS

Uruk-hai warriors march on the world of Men to destroy all who stand opposed to them. Vast numbers of these heavily armoured warriors, who excel at hand-to-hand combat, are in the Last March of the Ents (scenario 8) and The Battle For Helm's Deep (scenarios 13-17).

URUK-HAI

- **Armour:** Tin Bitz, Chainmail
- **Hair:** Chaos Black, Codex Grey
- **Leather:** Scorched Brown, Bestial Brown
- **Skin:** Dark Flesh, Dark Flesh/Bleached Bone

BATCH PAINTING

All Uruk-hai have a unified appearance. Rather than paint each warrior individually, choose a specific colour then apply that to as many models as you like, before going on to the next one. This is called Batch Painting and is useful when painting lots of identical looking models.

There are a huge variety of troops, from the Uruk-hai to the Berserkers and the siege troops, but despite their apparent different battlefield roles, they can all be painted in the same way.

BANNER

Use Skull White to paint the outline of a rough hand shape.

Then fill in the outline.

Finally, smooth down the shapes with Chaos Black.

ISENGARD TROLL

SCALES

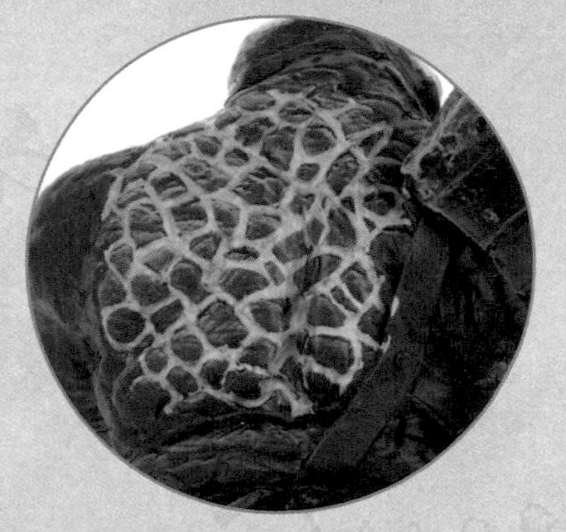

Over Chaos Black, wash the back with a thin mix of Dwarf Flesh and Codex Grey.

Once dry, drybrush the scales with Codex Grey.

Apply a mix of Chaos Black and Dwarf Flesh as a basecoat.

Next, apply a layer of Dwarf Flesh mixed with Codex Grey.

Finally, apply a final highlight of Bleached Bone.

SIEGE MACHINES

Both the Siege Assault Ballista and the Battering Ram are made from wood hewn from the trees of Fangorn and metal from the forges of Isengard. Paint the wood using Dark Flesh and Bestial Brown and the metal to match the Uruk-hai armour.

ELF WARRIORS

The Elves arrive to stand with the Men of Rohan against the forces of Isengard. They are skilled with both the bow and the sword, and are alternative forces for use in The Battle For Helm's Deep (scenarios 13-17).

ELF WARRIORS

Bows and sword handles: Scorched Brown, Dark Flesh

Cloaks: Shadow Grey/Chaos Black, Shadow Grey

Hair: Snakebite Leather/ Codex Grey, Bleached Bone

Inner robes: Scorched Brown, Bronzed Flesh

Red armour: Scab Red, Brown Ink

Scale mail: Shining Gold, Flesh Wash

Skin: Dwarf Flesh, Elf Flesh

GOLD ARMOUR

Paint with a mix of Boltgun Metal and Brazen Brass.

Add Shining Gold to the original mix and apply.

Then apply a mix of Black Ink and Dark Green Ink.

Highlight with Burnished Gold and Mithril Silver.

GANDALF THE WHITE

Gandalf the White aids Théoden against the forces of Isengard. He is one of the most potent Wizards in Middle-earth and commands the reinforcements at the Siege of Helm's Deep (scenario 17).

GANDALF

Hair and staff: Fortress Grey, Skull White

Flesh: Tanned Flesh, Dwarf Flesh

White Undercoat

Although layers of colour from grey to white can be built up over a black undercoat, a white one works better for painting light colours.

ROBES

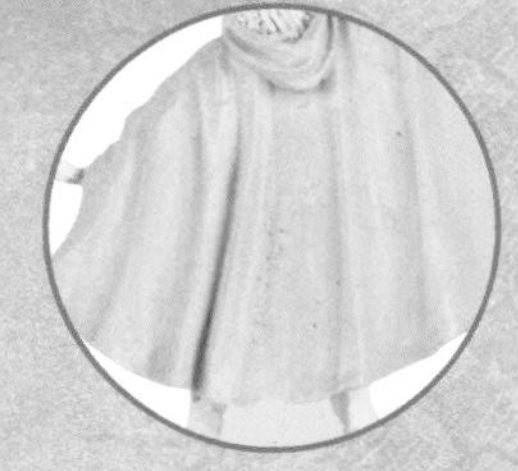

Basecoat Bleached Bone over a Skull White undercoat.

Then shade with Graveyard Earth.

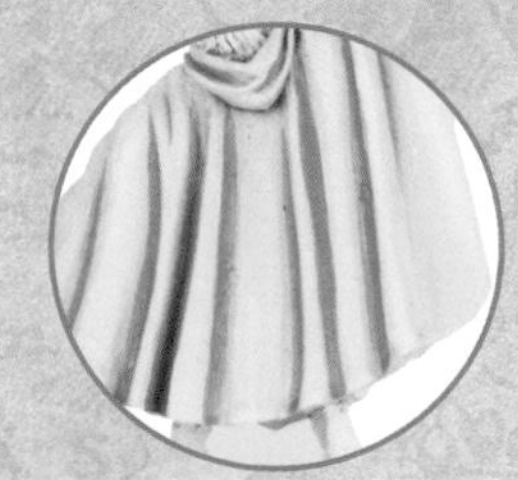

Next, add a highlight of Bleached Bone.

Finally, highlight with Skull White.

THE DEEPING WALL

The main thrust of the Uruk-hai's attack is against the Deeping Wall, defended by Aragorn, Legolas and Gimli, the Men of Rohan and Haldir's Elves. Its only weakness is the culvert that Saruman exploits to terrible advantage. This is a good piece to start with as you'll use many of the same techniques when building the other parts of the castle, including the battlements and the brickwork, as well as weathering effects.

MATERIALS

- 5 or 10mm foamboard
- Thick card
- Polystyrene foam
- Ready-mix filler
- Pins
- PVA glue
- Textured paint

1. Cut the following parts from 5mm foamboard: one front wall (200x130mm) and one back wall (200x105mm).

2. Cut one floor section (200x50mm) and one battlement strip (200x25mm).

3. Cut out two side walls (100x50mm).

4. Mark three equally spaced firing slots, 5mm wide and 25mm deep, onto the battlement strip.

5. Glue the side walls to the back wall. Use pins to secure the model whilst drying, and remove them afterwards.

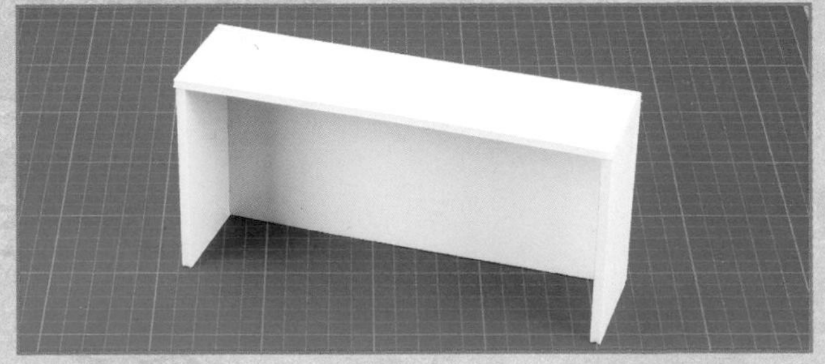

6. Glue the top in place onto the side walls and against the back wall.

7. Once the model is dry, glue the front wall in place and attach the battlement strip.

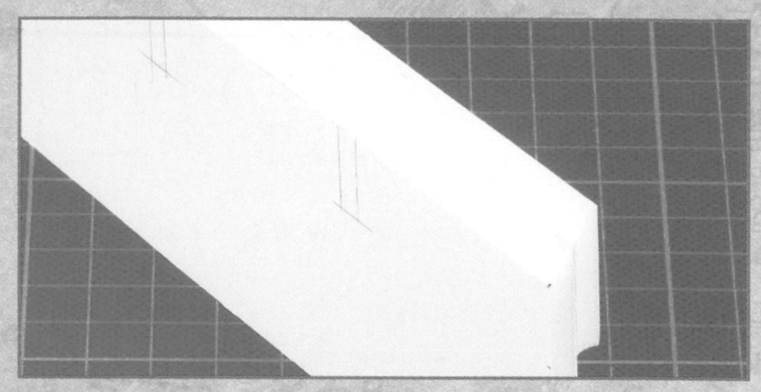

8. To make a bevelled battlement, mark a line 10mm from the top edge and cut along the line at an angle.

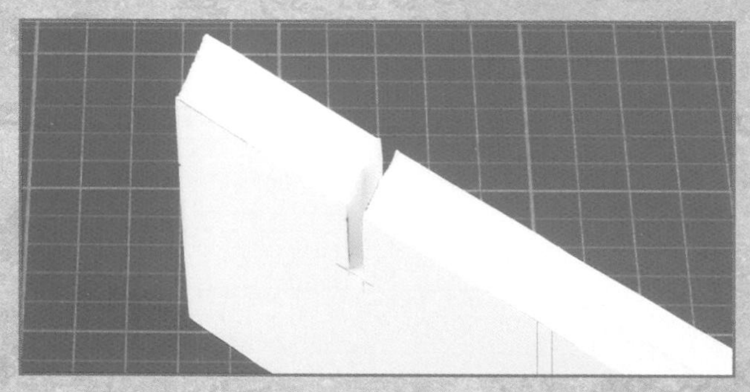

9. Cut out the firing slots, through both layers of foamboard and the bevelled edge.

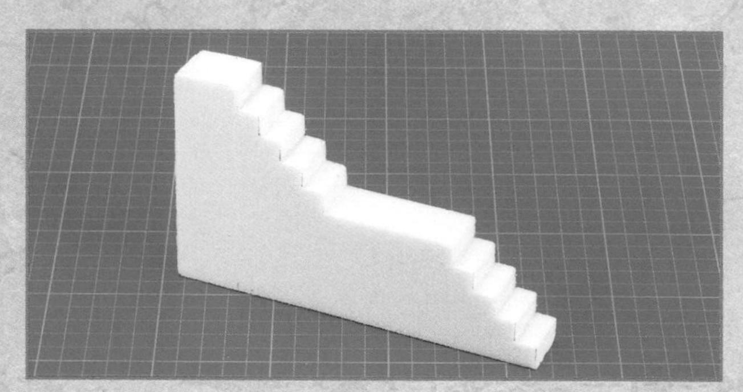

10. Using polystyrene foam, cut a stair section 30mm wide and 105mm high.

11. Glue this to the wall. Finally, create brickwork by gluing 15x10mm card rectangles to the wall.

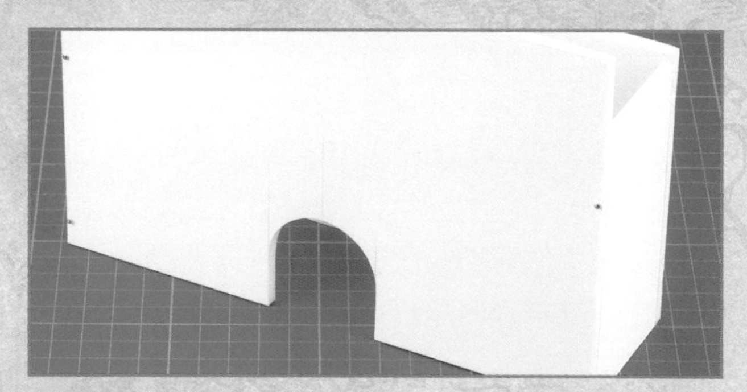

Alternative Stage. To add a culvert, cut out an archway at stage 7. This section of the wall has no stairs.

PAINTING HELM'S DEEP

1. Start by drybrushing Dark Angels Green along the base of the walls.

2. Then build up the stone colour by drybrushing on Codex Grey.

3. Continue with a drybrush of Fortress Grey.

4. Finish the walls by drybrushing patches of Rotting Flesh.

BREACHED WALL

Using his terrible magics, Saruman creates an explosive powder and has it poured into metal casings. Evading the deadly bowfire of the Elves, these are carried by Uruk-hai siege troops into the culvert underneath the Deeping Wall. With a torch carried by a Berserker, the Uruks succeed in blowing a huge hole in the Deeping Wall, to the horror of the defenders. The broken wall is a single piece model that replaces the Deeping Wall section with the culvert.

MATERIALS

- 5 or 10mm foamboard
- Thick card
- Polystyrene foam
- Ready-mix filler
- Pins
- PVA glue
- Textured paint

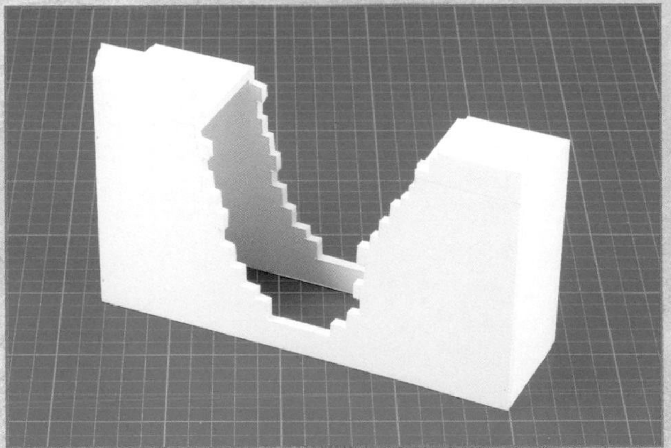

1. Start by making a complete Deeping Wall section and cut out a breached section from the piece.

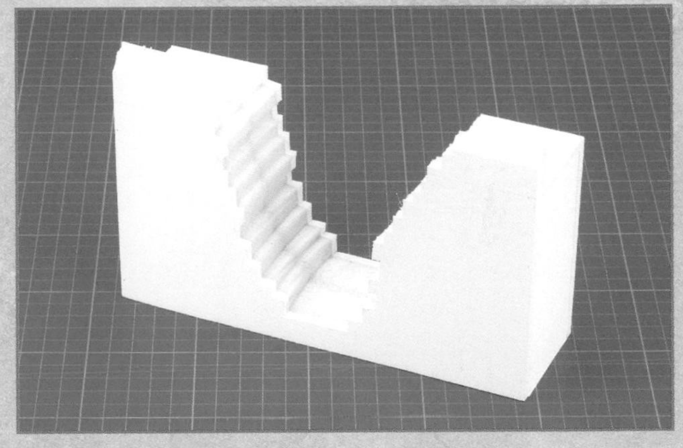

2. Fill this breach with polystyrene foam then use a hot wire cutter to carve rough block shapes.

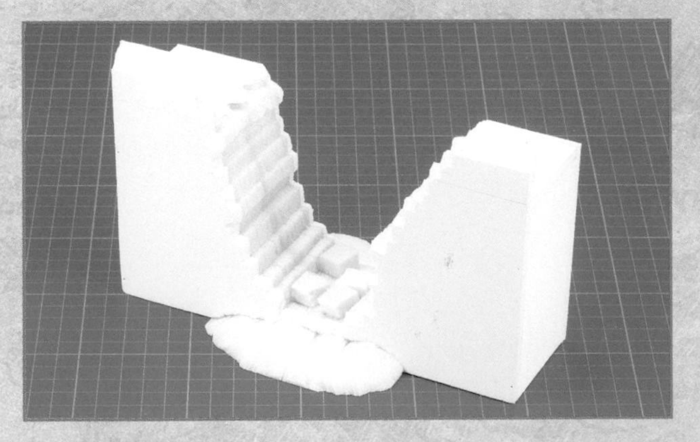

3. Add small scraps of polystyrene to the base of the wall and create brickwork as before.

4. Texture and paint the wall to match your other Deeping Wall sections.

SCENARIO 13

THE DEEPING WALL

The host of Isengard is come to Helm's Deep. Orcs and evil Men united under the banner of the White Hand march towards the last refuge of Rohan with naught but murder on their minds. For the Orcs it is the lust for battle and shedding of Mannish blood that drives them, while the Men of Dunland are driven to avenge themselves against those they blame for casting them from their homes hundreds of years before. King Théoden of Rohan has drawn his people into the caves behind the fortress and set his warriors to man the defences. As night falls and thunder splits the sky, hundreds of torches light the darkness and the host of Saruman's warriors come into view. The people of Rohan know that Helm's Deep has never been taken by force and cling to the hope that the Hornburg shall never fall so long as Men defend it...

PARTICIPANTS

GOOD

Aragorn with Andúril and armour
Legolas with armour and Elven cloak
Gimli with Elven cloak
Hama
8 Warriors of Rohan with throwing spear and shield
8 Warriors of Rohan with shield
8 Warriors of Rohan with bow

EVIL

1 Uruk-hai Captain with two-handed weapon
1 Dunlending Chieftain with two-handed weapon
10 Uruk-hai with pikes
10 Uruk-hai with shield
3 Uruk-hai Berserkers
2 Uruk-hai with banners
6 Dunlendings with two-handed axes
6 Dunlendings with shield
6 Dunlendings with bows
3 Uruk-hai Demolition Teams
1 Uruk-hai Siege Assault Ballista
The Evil force includes 4 ladders.

LAYOUT

This scenario is played on a board 24"/56cm by 48"/112cm. The Deeping Wall runs the length of the board 12"/28cm from the board edge, with a culvert in the exact centre of the wall. There are stairs on the inside of the wall as shown on the map. The ground before the walls is largely barren and empty, but you can place the odd patch of low scrub or rocks across the valley floor (see map).

"This is the hour when we draw swords together."

Aragorn, The Two Towers

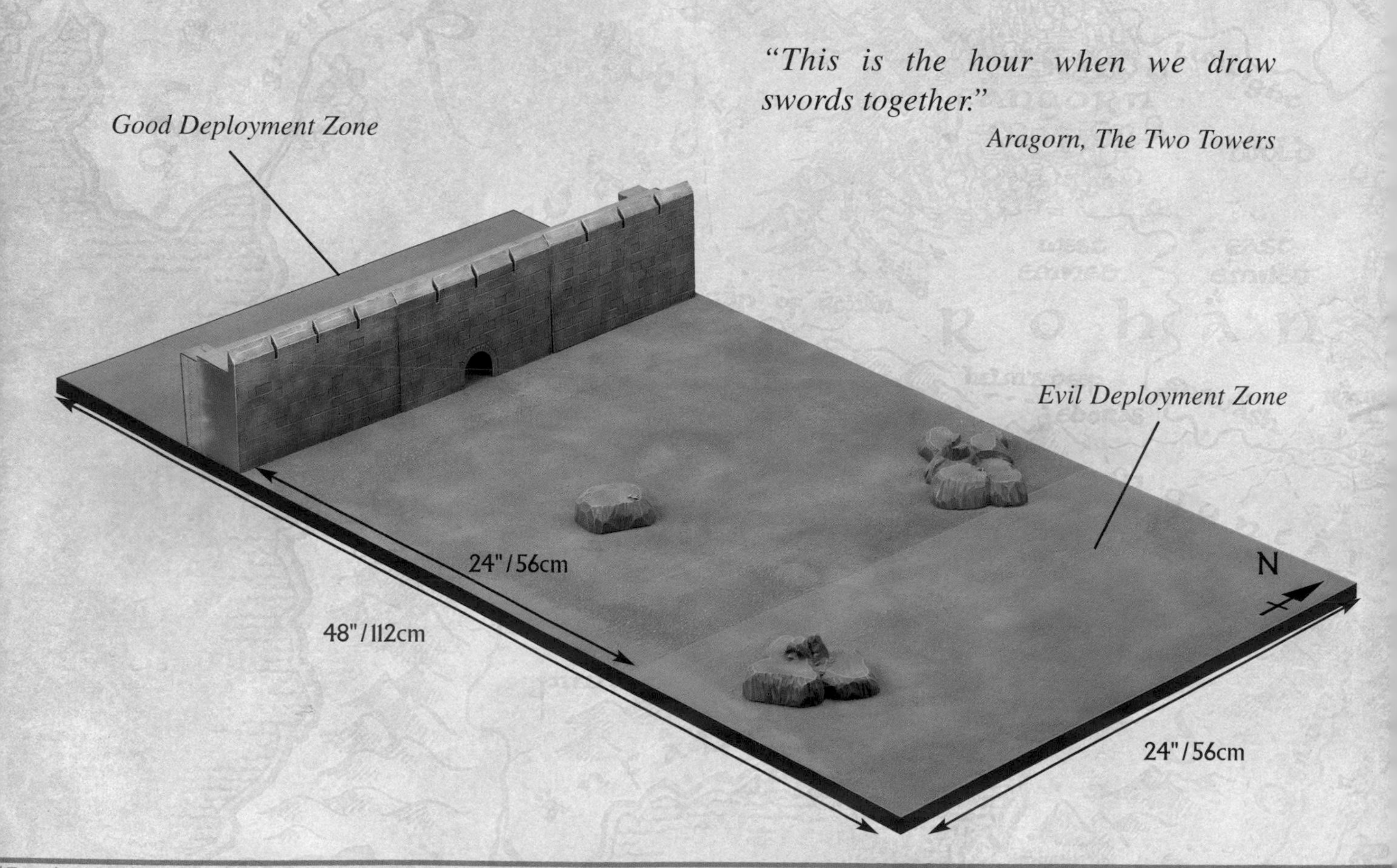

STARTING POSITIONS

Place all the Good models on or behind the Deeping Wall, then deploy the Evil force no closer than 24"/56cm to the wall.

OBJECTIVES

The Evil player must breach the Deeping Wall and get as many of his warriors into the fortress as possible before the end of the game. The Good player wins if he manages to break the Evil force. The Evil player wins if, at the end of any turn, there are 10 or more Evil models on the Good side of the Deeping Wall – note that this does not mean on the battlements, but actually in the courtyard on the other side of the wall.

SPECIAL RULES

The wall has but one weakness. The culvert is the weakest part of the wall and demolition charges placed there will do a terrific amount of damage. Demolition charges that explode in the culvert always count as having rolled a 6 on the Detonation chart (titanic explosion).

Scenario note. To play the scenario as it appears in the film, swap 8 Warriors of Rohan with bow for 8 Elf warriors with light armour and Elf bow. In addition, swap Háma for Haldir with armour and an Elf bow.

POINTS MATCH

Good (550 points)

Must include three Heroes. No Hero may be mounted on a steed. No more than a third of the Good force may be armed with bows of any kind.

Evil (850 points)

Must include two Heroes. No models may be mounted on steeds and no more than a third of the Evil force may be armed with bows of any kind. No more than one siege engine may be included.

SCENARIO 14

INTO THE BREACH

The Deeping Wall is breached! The Orcs have with them a blasting fire that has ripped the living rock from its foundations in a crash of flame and smoke. The rubble of the Deeping Wall is thrown skywards and comes crashing down in a rain of rocky debris. As the smoke clears, a wide breach is revealed in the wall and the Uruk-hai warriors and their Dunlending allies pour inside in an effort to overwhelm the defenders in one fell swoop. But hope yet remains, for Aragorn and Gimli rally the defenders to push the enemy from Helm's Deep. Can the Men of Rohan and their allies hurl back the enemy before it is too late?

PARTICIPANTS

GOOD

Aragorn with Andúril and armour
Éomer
Captain of Rohan with heavy armour and shield
Gimli with Elven cloak
8 Warriors of Rohan with throwing spear and shield
8 Warriors of Rohan with bow
8 Warriors of Rohan with shield
1 Warrior of Rohan with banner

EVIL

2 Uruk-hai Captains with shield
1 Dunlending Chieftain with two-handed weapon
3 Dunlending Warriors with bow
3 Dunlending Warriors with shield
10 Uruk-hai with pike
10 Uruk-hai with shield
6 Uruk-hai Berserkers
2 Uruk-hai with banner
1 Isengard Troll

LAYOUT

The scenario is played on a board 24"/56cm by 24"/56cm. This scenario takes place in the ruins of the Deeping Wall that has been breached by the devilry of Saruman. Place the Deeping Wall 6"/14cm from the eastern board edge, with a breach, roughly 3"/8cm wide in the exact centre. Each intact wall section has a stairway leading to the ground. Place scattered rocky outcrops around the breach to represent rubble from the explosion (see map).

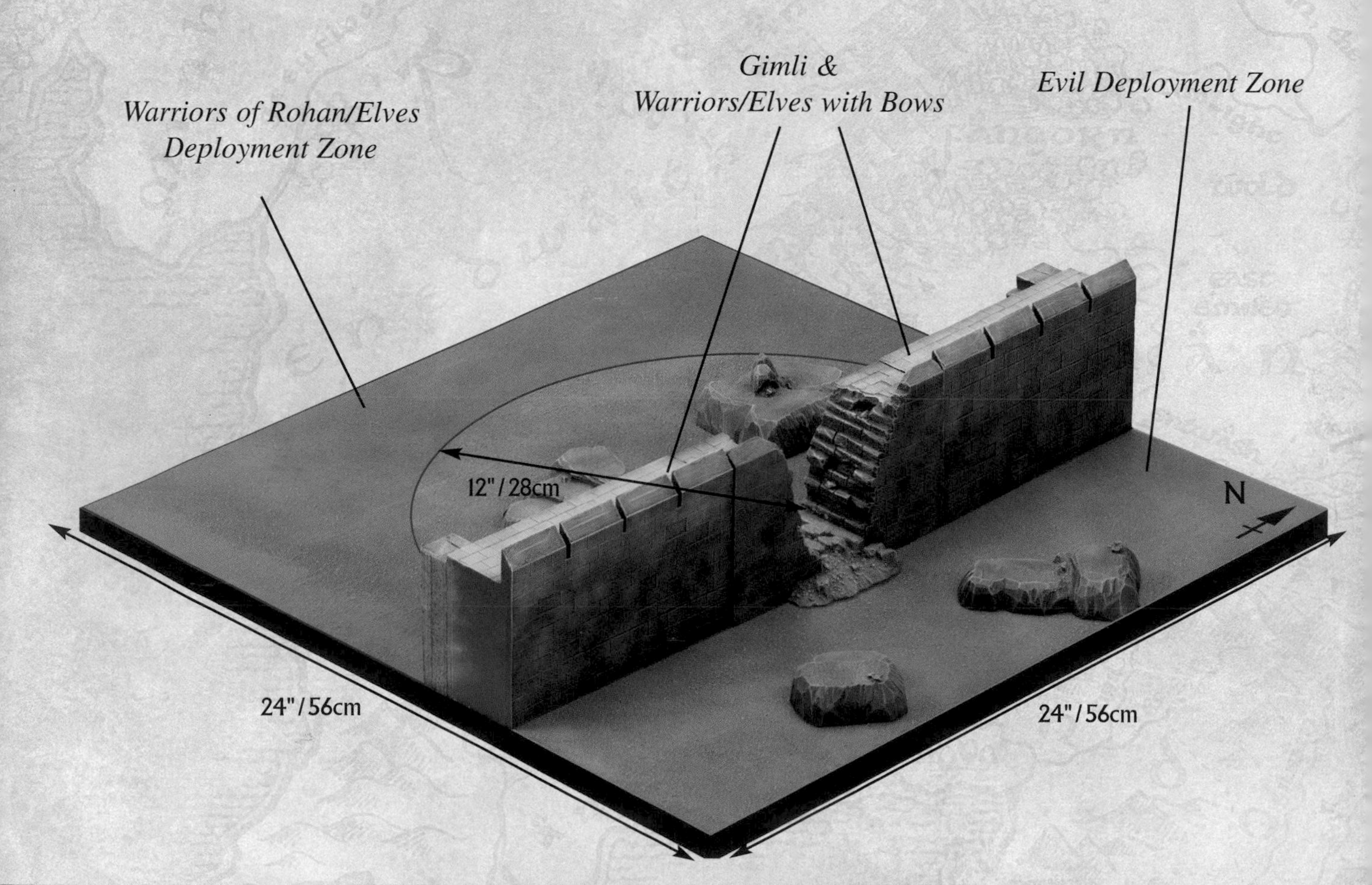

STARTING POSITIONS

Place Gimli and the Warriors of Rohan with bows on the Deeping Wall. Next, deploy the Evil force anywhere on the breach or on the eastern side of the wall, though no Evil models may be within the fortress or on the walls. Place Aragorn inside the fortress at least 6"/14cm from the breach and then place the remainder of the Warriors of Rohan and the Captain of Rohan inside the fortress at least 12"/ 28cm from the breach.

OBJECTIVES

The Uruk-hai seek to overwhelm the defenders of the Deeping Wall in one, overwhelming hammer-blow then sweep onwards to the Hornburg. The Evil player wins if there at least a third of his starting number of models inside the fortress 6"/14cm from the walls during the End phase of any turn. The Good player wins if he can prevent this.

SPECIAL RULES

Earthshaking Blast. The force of the explosion means that all the Warriors of Rohan on the Deeping Wall begin the game lying down, though Gimli's stout Dwarf legs allow him to keep his feet and he deploys as normal.

Ruined walls. The inside faces of the breach are rugged and rough, with plenty of handholds and places to climb. They may be climbed by a model making a successful Climb check.

Scenario note. If you want to play the film version of this scenario, simply substitute Haldir for Éomer, the Captain of Rohan for an Elf Captain and substitute all the Warriors of Rohan for 8 Elf Warriors with light armour and Elven blade, 8 Elf Warriors with light armour and Elf bow (who start the game on the Deeping Wall).

POINTS MATCH

Good (600 points)

Must include at least two heroes to take the place of Aragorn and Gimli. No more than half the Good force may be equipped with bows of any kind and no models may be mounted.

Evil (600 points)

Must include at least two Heroes and no more than a third of the Evil force may be equipped with bows. No Evil models may be mounted.

THE GATEHOUSE

With the Deeping Wall in ruins and the Elves in retreat, the huge gatehouse of Helm's Deep comes under attack by the Uruk-hai carrying huge battering rams – they finally smash through the gate and desperate fighting breaks out. Using all the techniques covered previously to make the Deeping Wall, we now show how to build the mighty gatehouse and its distinctive shape. Balsa wood is used to make the gate as well as additional defences on the gatehouse's walls.

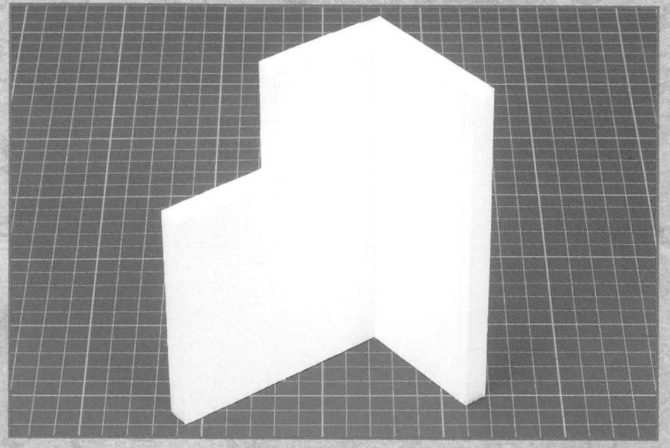

1. Cut rectangles 150x72mm and another 150x100mm (with a 50mm square cut in one corner) from 10mm foamboard. Glue them together.

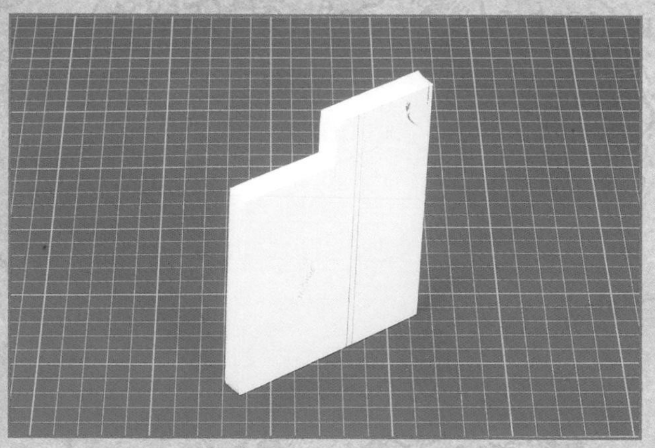

2. Cut a 120x95mm piece of foamboard with 20x45mm cut from one corner.

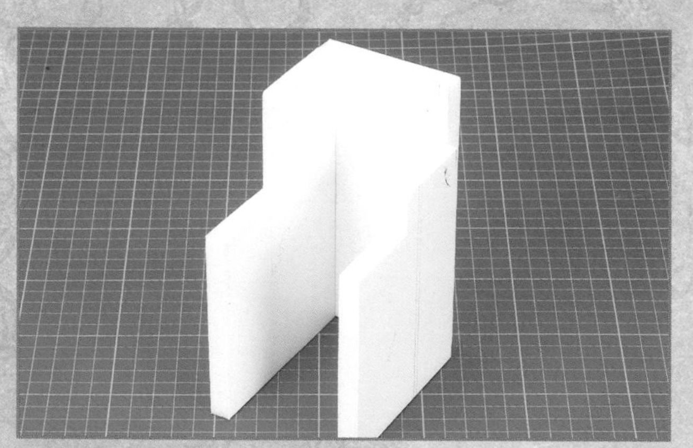

3. Glue this piece to the front wall 5mm in.

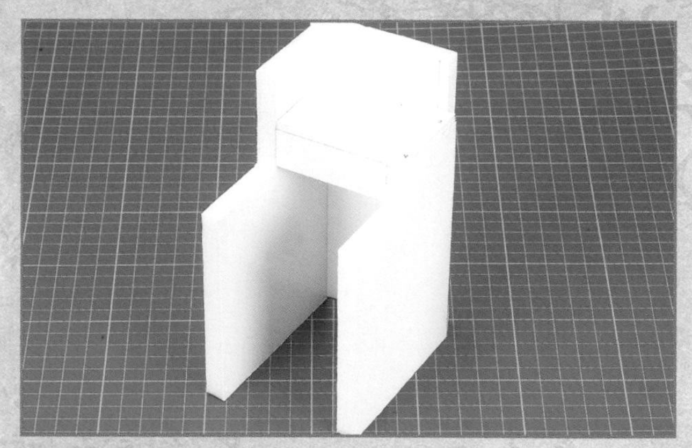

4. Make the floor (67x50mm) and a ledge (56x20mm) from 5mm foamboard.

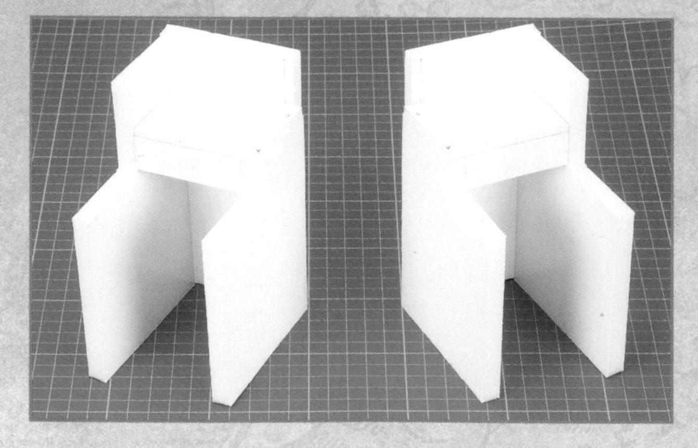

5. With the first tower complete, make another but this time a mirrored version.

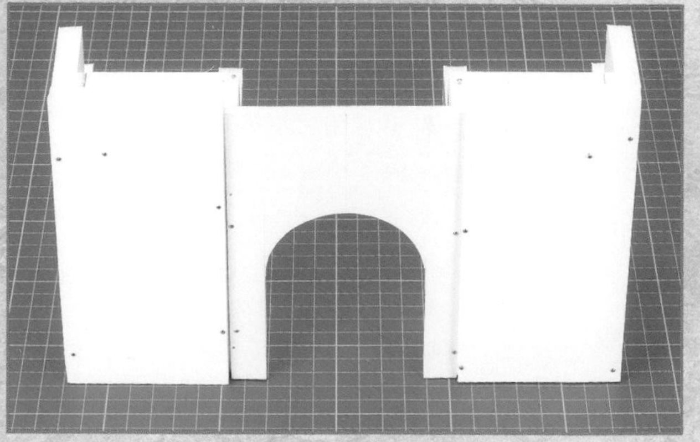

6. Make an archway 140x100mm with an arch 90x70mm. Glue it between the two towers.

7. Cut another archway 25x100mm then glue it to the rear of the towers.

8. Make a floor 245x100mm, and cut out sections to match the existing corners.

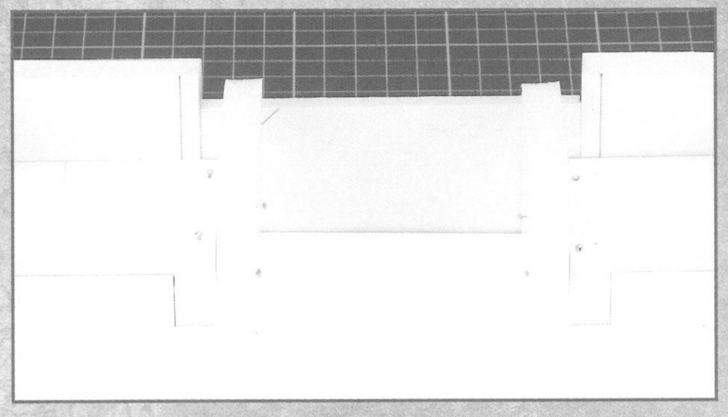

9. Using 10mm foamboard, cut two pieces 50x45mm; glue these to the inside edge.

10. Cut two pieces 25x10mm; glue these to the outer corners of the tower.

11. Then cut two pieces 45x10mm from 5mm foamboard and glue them to either end of the towers.

12. Make four steps (two 25x10mm and two 25x5mm). Glue in place and buttress with 25x10mm triangular strips.

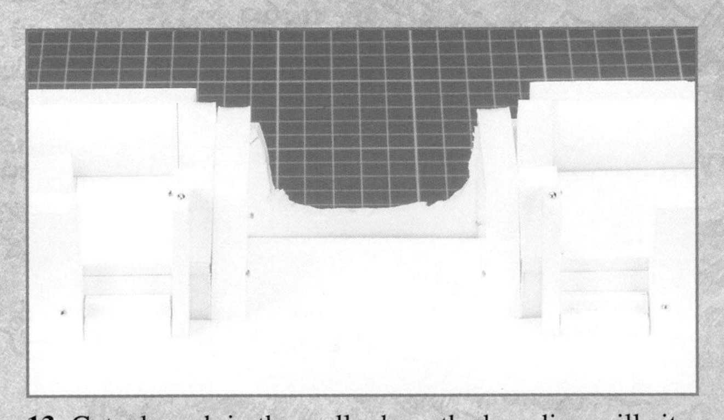

13. Cut a breach in the wall where the hoarding will sit.

14. Texture and paint the gatehouse in the same way as the Deeping Wall.

THE GATE

1. Cut a piece of balsa wood to fit the gate and score with 5mm planks.

2. To make layered metalwork for the gates first draw their outlines onto thin card.

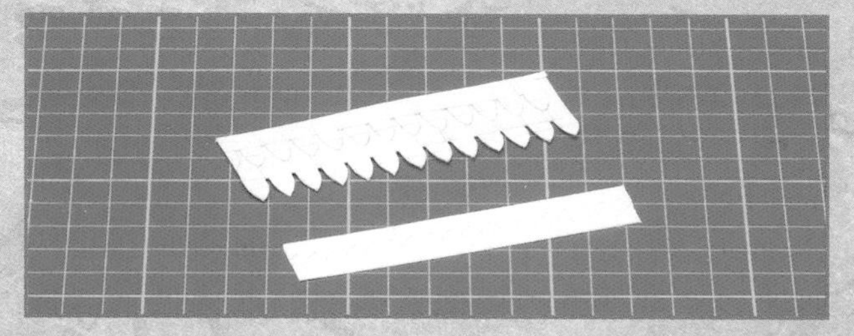

3. Cut out the shapes then layer them on top of each other.

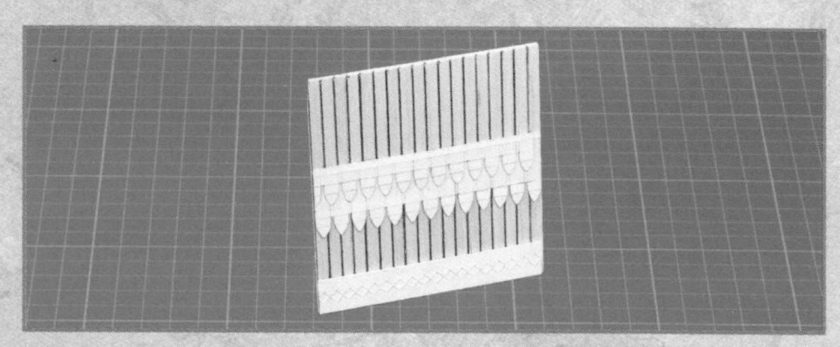

4. Once dry, attach the two finished pieces to the gate.

5. Cut a couple of balsa wood strips and glue them to the back of the gate.

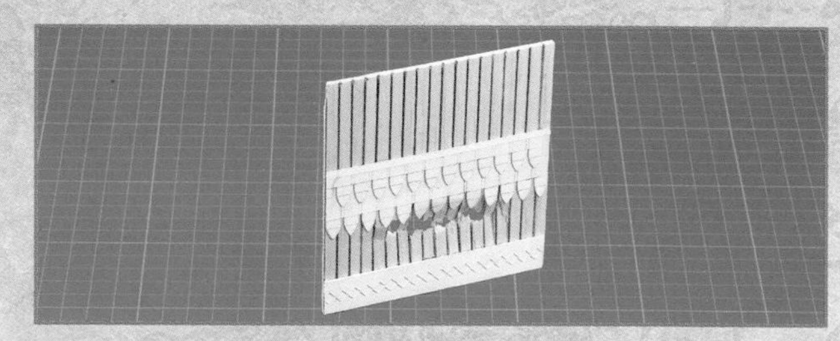

6. Then cut through the balsa wood and carefully break a hole through the gate. Finish to match your Rohan houses.

HOARDING

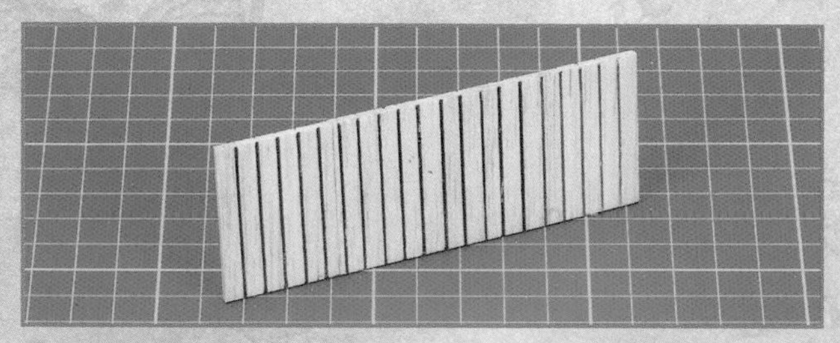

1. Cut a piece of balsa wood 105x40mm and score 5mm planks with a pencil.

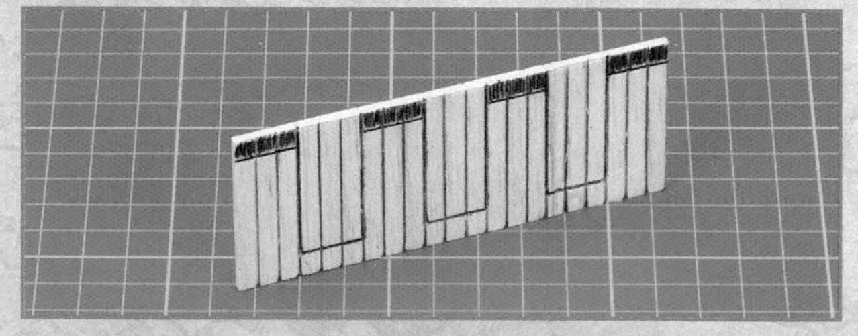

2. Mark three shutters onto the hoarding-5mm from the bottom and top.

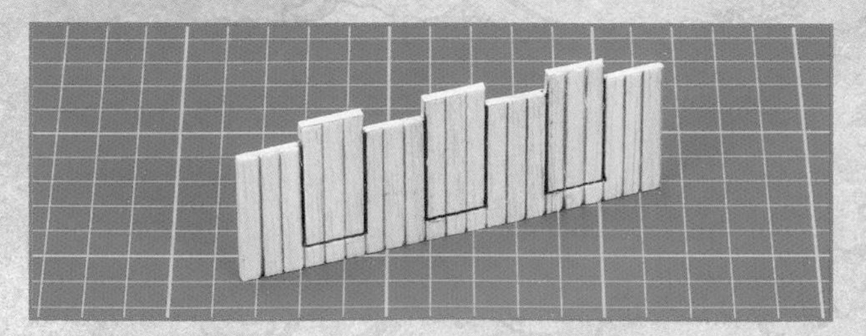

3. Cut away the balsa wood to create the effect of shutters.

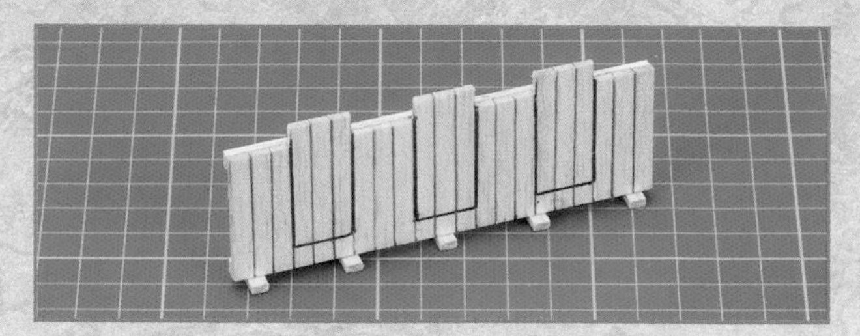

4. Glue strips of balsa wood top and bottom-glue smaller pieces along the bottom and paint to match the gate.

THE CAUSEWAY

Leading up to the gatehouse is a curved causeway, wide enough for four warriors abreast. With their shields held above their heads, the Uruk-hai march up the causeway and cover the battering ram as it is hurled against the wooden gate.

1. Cut two pieces of polystyrene 210x160mm then glue them together and mark a diagonal line along both edges.

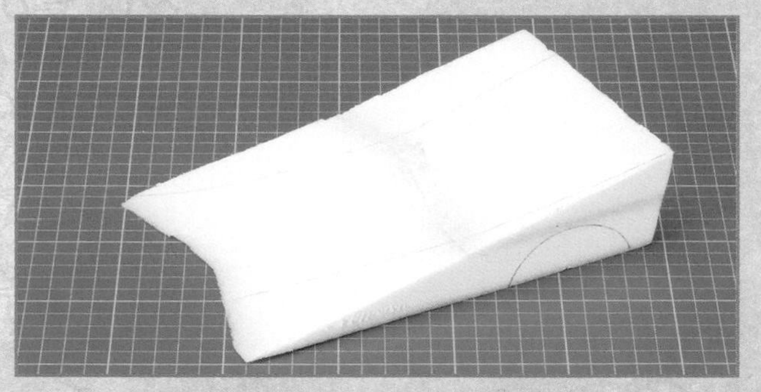

2. Carefully cut along the line with a hot-wire cutter, then mark out curved causeway 100mm wide on top and the culvert on the sides.

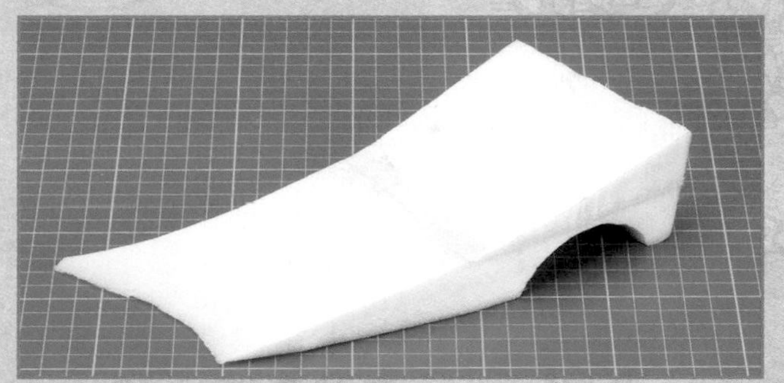

3. Cut out first the culvert and then the curve of the causeway, and paint and detail the piece to match the Deeping Wall.

RAISED HELM'S DEEP

For In The Shadow Of The Hornburg (Scenario 15) you will need to raise Helm's Deep on a rocky outcrop. Use your Helm's Deep gateway and causeway to mark out an outline on polystyrene foam, and cut it to match. Sculpt, texture and paint these rocks to match the craggy hills built earlier. Théoden Rides Out (Scenario 16) and The Siege of Helm's Deep (Scenario 17) also require the curved walls to be raised, so repeat the process using your curved walls as a template.

SCENARIO 15

IN THE SHADOW OF THE HORNBURG

The battle for Helm's Deep goes ill for the defenders. The Deeping Wall is breached and enemy warriors pour into the courtyard. Now the Hornburg gate is assailed by Uruk-hai carrying battering rams and protected by a wall of shields. Though the defenders rain arrows and rocks upon them, there are always more to replace the slain. The booming thud of ram upon gate echoes through the Hornburg and all within know it is a matter of moments until the gate is smashed to ruin. Seeing the gate's peril, Aragorn and Gimli make haste through a postern and come upon the Uruk-hai from the flanks, scattering them like wheat before the scythe. The defenders have been granted a respite, but Uruk-hai Captains and Dunlending Chieftains gather their warriors for yet another charge. Can Aragorn and Gimli hold the causeway long enough for the defenders to shore up the gate?

PARTICIPANTS

GOOD

Aragorn with Andúril and armour
Gimli with Elven cloak

EVIL

1 Uruk-hai Captain with heavy armour and shield
1 Dunlending Chieftain with two-handed weapon
3 Dunlending Warriors with two-handed weapon
3 Dunlending Warriors with shield
1 Dunlending Warrior with banner
10 Uruk-hai Warriors with shield
5 Uruk-hai Berserkers

LAYOUT

The scenario is played on a board 12"/28cm by 15"/36cm. This scenario takes place before the damaged gate of the Hornburg. Place the gate section in the centre of the western board edge. The causeway is 4"/10cm wide and runs from the gateway towards the eastern board edge (see map).

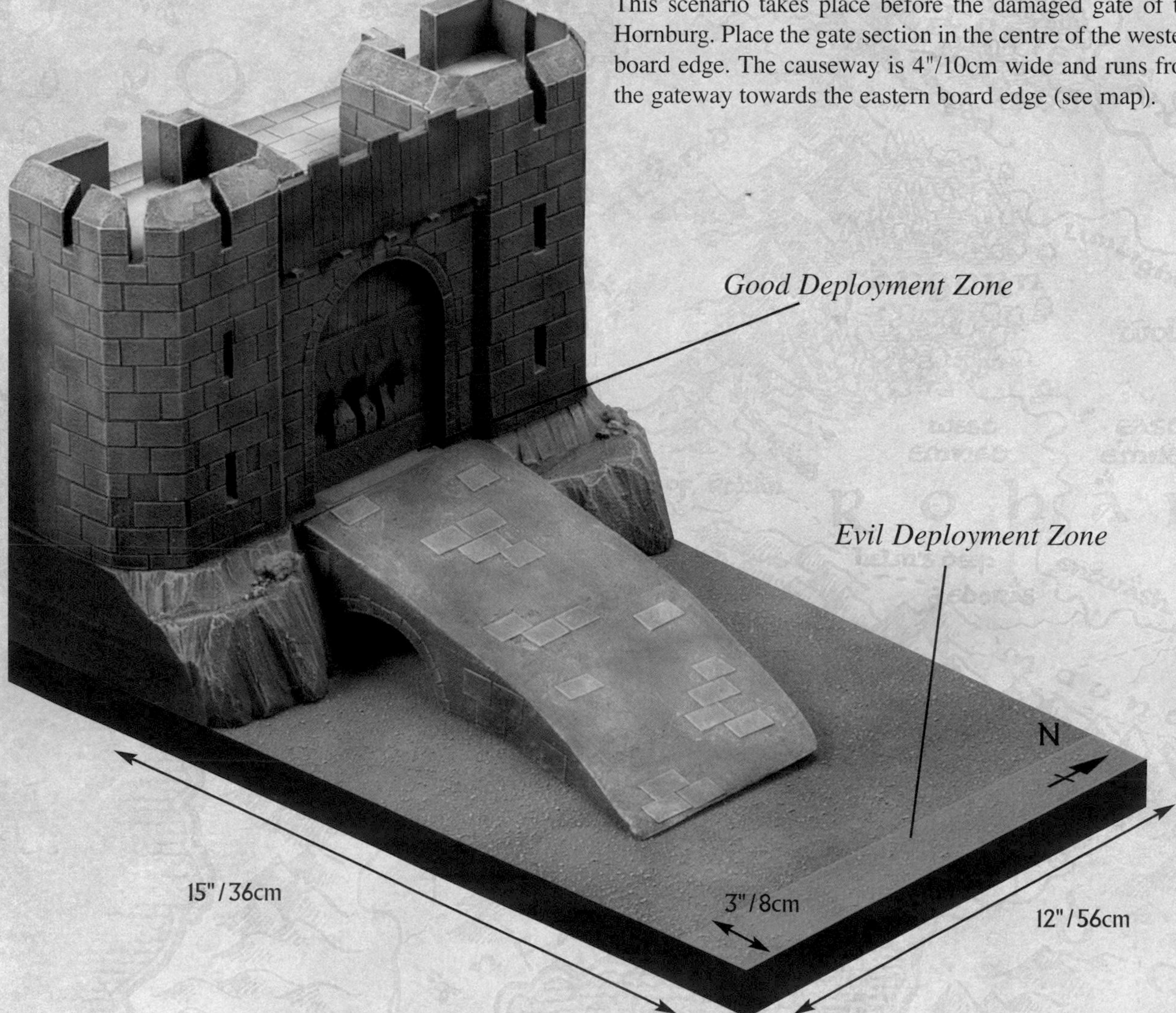

STARTING POSITIONS

The Good player sets up Aragorn and Gimli touching the gate and the Evil player then deploys the Uruk-hai up to 3"/8cm from the eastern table edge.

POINTS MATCH

Good (300 points)

Must consist entirely of Heroes, none of whom may be mounted or carry bows.

Evil (400 points)

Must include at least two Heroes. None of the Evil force may be mounted or be equipped with bows.

OBJECTIVES

The Evil player must try and break down the gate to the Hornburg and get as many of his models through as possible. The Evil player wins if he is able to move at least six models off the table through the gateway by the end of turn 10 or kill both Good Heroes. The Good player wins if he manages to prevent this. Note that Evil models removed from the table in this way still count towards the Evil force's numbers when checking for whether or not it is Broken.

SPECIAL RULES

The Gate: The gate to the Hornburg has been heavily damaged by Uruk-hai rammers and is splintered and nearly broken open by the time Aragorn and Gimli arrive. As a result, the gate only has a Defence value of 8 and a single Batter Point remaining.

SCENARIO 16

THÉODEN RIDES OUT

Though the Men of Rohan and their Elven allies have fought gallantly, Helm's Deep is lost. Heroic deeds and valiant hearts alone are not enough to turn aside such unthinking hate and now Orcs pour through the breach in the Deeping Wall and swarm the outer courtyard. King Théoden rankles against awaiting his fate within the halls of his fortress and resolves to make an ending that will make his forefathers proud. Readying his horse Snowmane, the King of Rohan and his remaining warriors prepare to ride out and meet the foe head on. Even as they charge from the gateway and cleave a path through the enemy, unexpected aid is riding towards Helm's Deep. Can Théoden and the heroes of the West survive long enough for their friends to reach them?

PARTICIPANTS

GOOD

Aragorn with Andúril and Armour
Théoden with heavy armour and armoured horse
Legolas with Elven cloak
Gamling with the Royal Standard of Rohan
Éomer
Erkenbrand
Gandalf the White on Shadowfax
3 Rohan Royal Guard with throwing spear
6 Riders of Rohan with throwing spear
12 Riders of Rohan
All Good models are mounted on horses

EVIL

3 Uruk-hai Captains with shield
1 Uruk-hai Shaman
1 Dunlending Chieftain with two-handed weapon
3 Dunlending Warriors with two-handed weapon
3 Dunlending Warriors with shield
3 Dunlending Warriors with bow
10 Uruk-hai with shield
2 Uruk-hai with banner
9 Uruk-hai with crossbow
10 Uruk-hai with pike
9 Uruk-hai Berserker
1 Isengard Troll

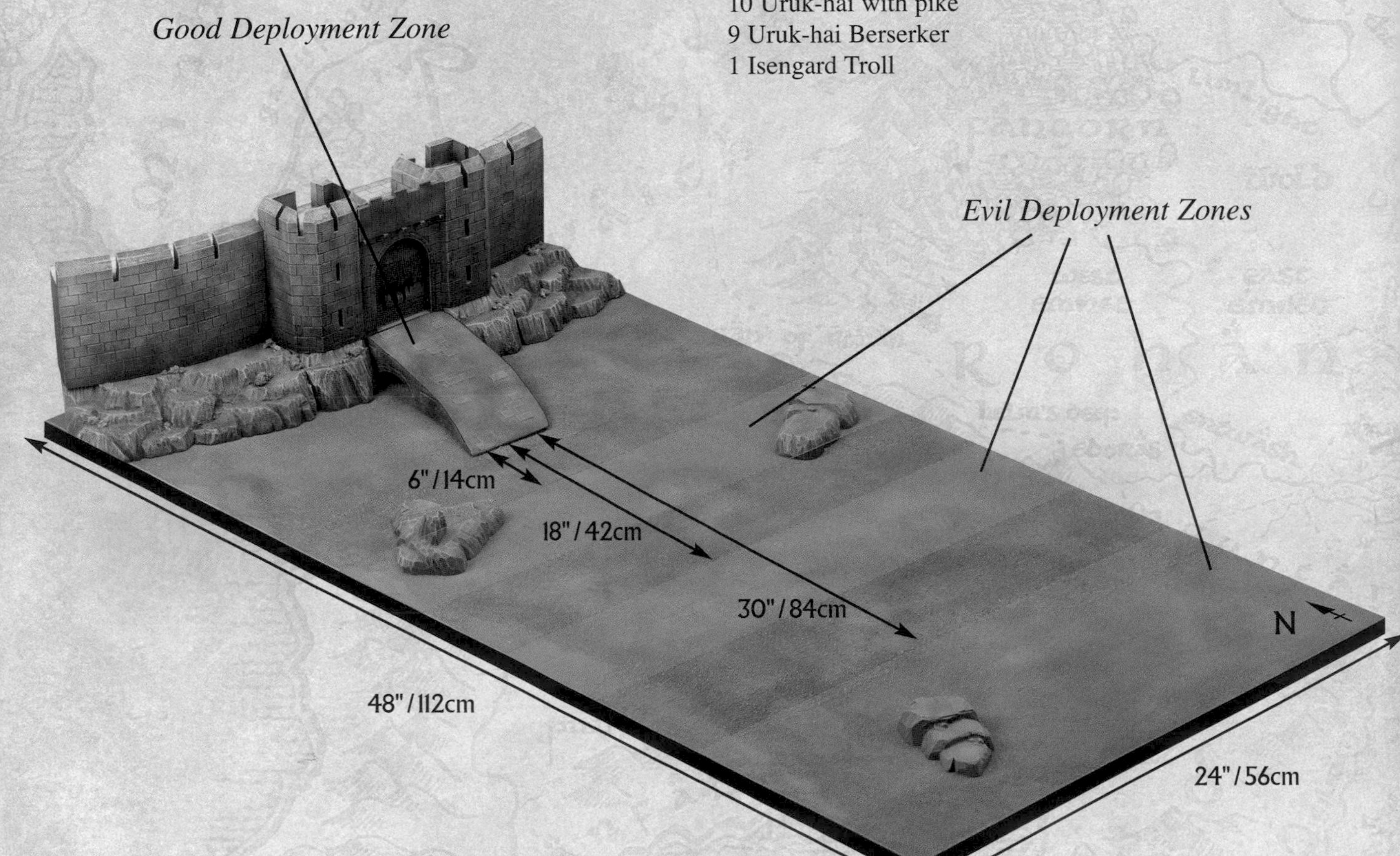

LAYOUT

The scenario is played on a board 24"/56cm by 48"/112cm. This scenario takes place before the walls of Helm's Deep. Place the walls of Helm's Deep across the southern board edge with the gateway section in the middle of the wall and the causeway in front of the gate. Scatter the valley floor with the occasional clusters of rocks (see map).

STARTING POSITIONS

Place Théoden, Éomer, Aragorn, Legolas, Gamling and the Rohan Royal Guard on the causeway. The rest of the Good force is not deployed to begin with and will become available during the course of the scenario. The evil player then divides his models into three roughly equal forces. He deploys one force (chosen by the Good player) between 6"/14cm and 12"/28cm of the bottom of the causeway. The second force is then deployed between 18"/42cm and 24"/56cm from the causeway. Finally, the third force is deployed at least 30"/84cm from the end of he causeway. No model may be deployed within 6"/14cm of an enemy model.

OBJECTIVES

The Good player wins if he manages to reduce the Evil side to less than a quarter of its starting number of models. The Evil player wins if he kills Théoden and any other three Good Heroes.

SPECIAL RULES

Dawn is come. As dawn breaks across the eastern horizon, Gandalf, Erkenbrand and the Riders of Rohan arrive to save the day, much to the shock and horror of the Uruk-hai. At the beginning of turn 5, roll a D6 – on a 4, 5 or 6, the remainder of the Good force moves on from any point on the eastern board edge during the Good player's Move phase. On a 1, 2 or 3 they have not yet arrived, so roll again next turn, adding one to the dice score. If they still do not arrive, then the rest of the Good force will automatically arrive in the Good player's Move phase of turn 7.

No Surrender. This is to be Théoden's last, defiant ride to glory and thus he and his warriors are filled with the courage of the ancient kings of Rohan. All Good models will automatically pass any Courage tests they are required to make.

Scenario Note. If you want to play this scenario as it appears in the film, simply take Erkenbrand out of the scenario and use Éomer in his role.

POINTS MATCH

Good (1,000 points)

Must include at least four Heroes, all of whom must be mounted. Nominate one Hero to take on the role of Théoden. Choose a third of the force to represent the warriors who arrive with Erkenbrand/Éomer. All models must be mounted on steeds.

Evil (1,100 Points)

Must include at least two Heroes. None of the Evil force may be mounted and no more than a third of the Evil force may be equipped with bows or crossbows.

CURVED WALL

Helm's Deep is a huge castle with curved walls and a massive fortified gatehouse in the centre. Its here that the fighting for Helm's Deep is the hardest, as the Uruks unleash their war machines against the ramparts. To help create the distinctive shape of the castle of Helm's Deep, make a pair of curved wall sections to go on either side. Making a curved section of wall is easier that it first appears as we demonstrate here.

MATERIALS

5 or 10mm foamboard
Thick card
A3 paper
Pins
PVA glue
Textured paint
Metal rules
Protractor

1. Draw a centre line on the paper. Attach a piece of string to a pencil and use it as a compass; Draw an arc at the top of the line, and another 50mm below.

2. Use the protractor to draw two lines 15° on either side of the centre line, up to the top of the sheet.

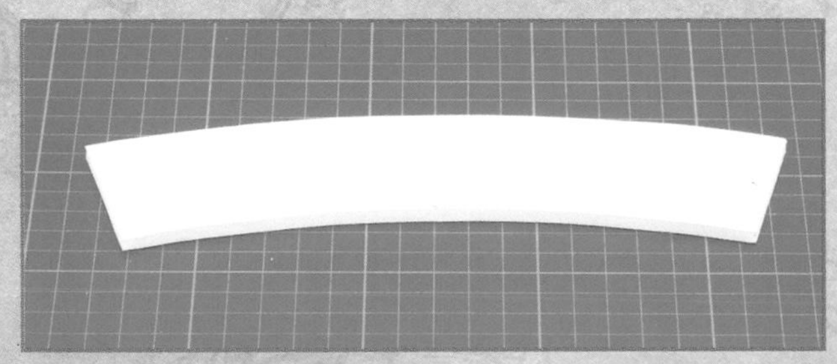

3. Cut around the outline to make a paper template, and then trace this shape onto foam board twice. Carefully cut out the shapes.

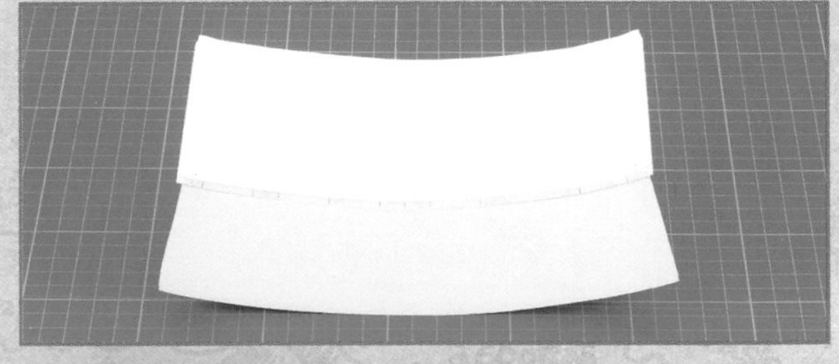

4. Make a rear wall from foam board 190x105mm. Score vertical lines 10mm apart, then glue to the curved floor section.

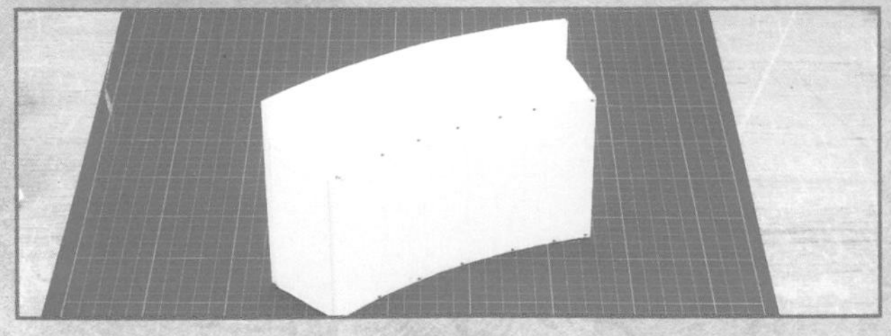

5. Glue the second curved wall on top with side walls cut to fit. Make a front wall 215x130mm and bend to fit as before.

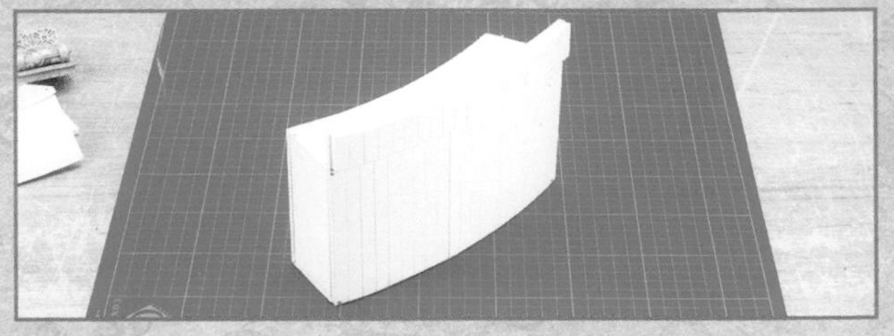

6. Build a battlement 215x25mm to fit the front wall. Glue it in place and finish the wall to match the rest of the castle.

COMPLETING HELM'S DEEP

Once you've made the Deeping Wall and the gatehouse, you'll have all the skills and techniques needed to complete the whole of Helm's Deep if you wish. To finish off we show all the pieces you'll need to make the whole fortress. The finished model will stretch across the whole of the four-foot square gaming board and looks very impressive.

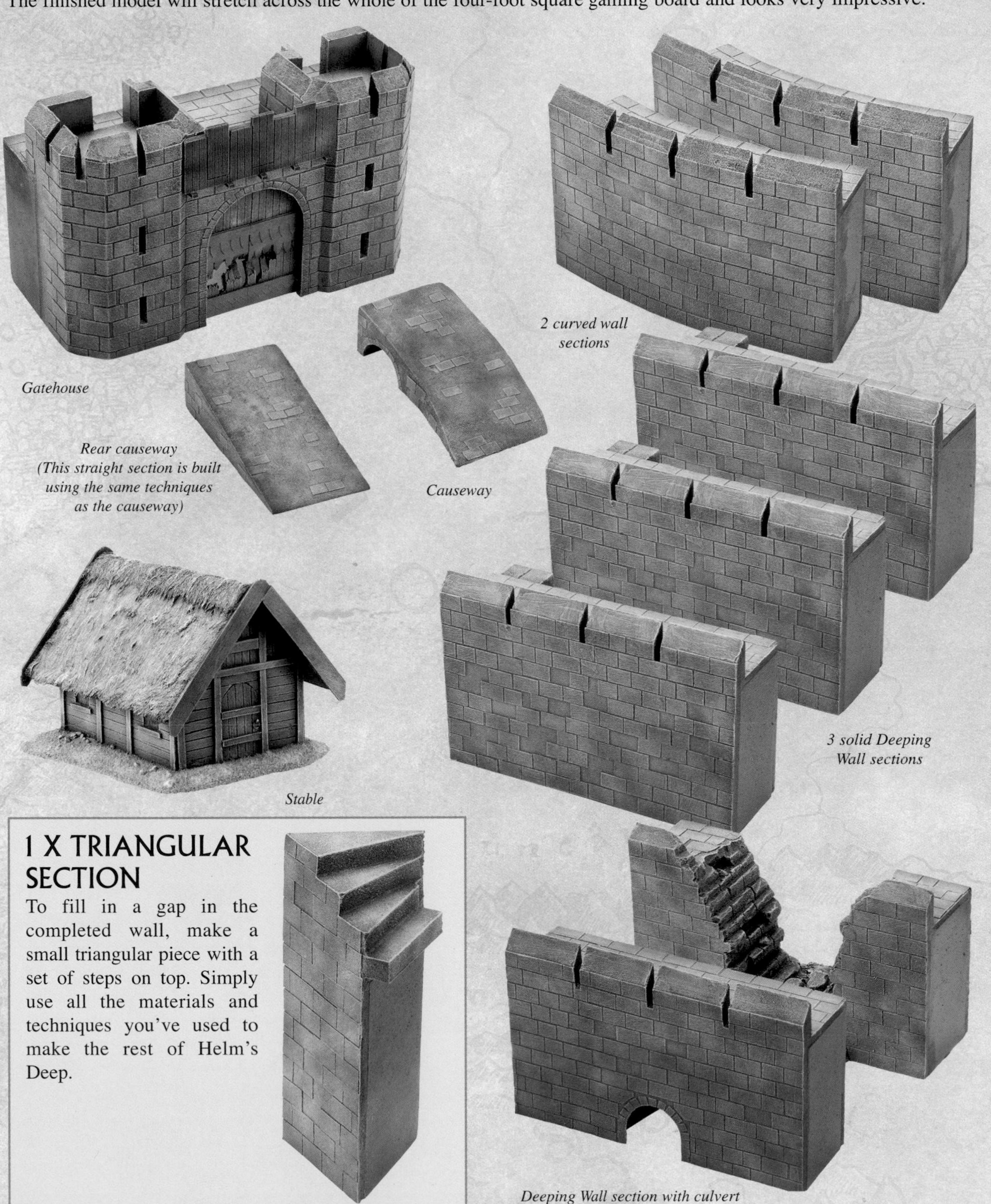

Gatehouse

Rear causeway (This straight section is built using the same techniques as the causeway)

Causeway

2 curved wall sections

Stable

3 solid Deeping Wall sections

1 X TRIANGULAR SECTION

To fill in a gap in the completed wall, make a small triangular piece with a set of steps on top. Simply use all the materials and techniques you've used to make the rest of Helm's Deep.

Deeping Wall section with culvert

THE SIEGE OF HELM'S DEEP

Why not fight the whole battle of Helm's Deep from beginning to end? If you get together with a couple of friends you could pool together your The Lord of The Rings miniatures collections and make an event out of it. Just make sure you have plenty of time and snacks to hand!

FORCES

Good: Choose 1,500 points of Good models, including Aragorn, Théoden, Legolas, Gimli and Gandalf the White.

Evil: Choose 1,500 points of Evil models including White Hand Uruk-hai, Dunlendings and Orcs. For every twenty models, the Evil side can include one ladder.

OBJECTIVES:

Good win: The Good player wins if the Evil force is wiped out and Aragorn, Gandalf and Théoden are still alive.

Evil win: The Evil player wins if Aragorn, Gandalf and Théoden are all slain, thus sealing the fate of Middle-earth.

Draw: The Evil force is wiped out, but has slain one or more of Aragorn, Gandalf and Théoden.

THE WHITE RIDER

Gandalf the White and the reinforcements deployed with him arrive at the end of the Good Move phase in turn 12. Remember, models that move onto the board cannot charge in the turn they arrive, but may otherwise act normally.

LEGION OF THE WHITE HAND

Every time an Evil warrior with a single Wound is slain, put it aside. At the end of the following Evil Move phase it may re-enter play on a dice roll of 3 or more. If a 1 or 2 is rolled, the model may not re-enter – do not roll for it again. Once Gandalf and the rest of Rohan's reinforcements arrive, no more Evil models may enter play.

The Evil force is only considered Broken at the beginning of any turn when there are less than 50 Evil models in play.

STARTING POSITIONS

The scenario is played on a board 48"/112cm by 48"/112cm.

Good: Choose at least 500 points of Good models (including Gandalf the White) for reinforcements. These are not deployed until later. Aragorn, Théoden, Legolas and Gimli and the remaining Good models are all deployed within the walls of Helm's Deep.

Evil: All Evil models are placed anywhere on the board no closer than 12"/28cm to the walls of Helm's Deep.

HELM'S DEEP HAS BUT ONE WEAKNESS

The culvert can be destroyed as described in scenario 12, The Deeping Wall. If demolition charges are used on other parts of the wall, they will have no effect though they can be used as normal to attack the gate.

THE GATE

At the start of the siege the gate is intact and braced from within. Treat it as a fortress gate, with a Defence of 10 and 3 Batter Points.

THÉODEN RIDES OUT

As long as Théoden is still alive, from turn 8 onwards any surviving Rohirrim may attempt to ride out of Helm's Deep in a glorious last charge. In the Move phase of turn 8 (and in each following turn) any Warrior or Hero of Rohan, Aragorn and Legolas may mount a horse by moving into base contact with the stable.

When this happens, treat any Warriors of Rohan that mount horses as Riders of Rohan from that point forwards. If Gamling does this, he may be equipped with the Banner of Rohan.

Note: Théoden must join the charge, otherwise no Good model may mount a horse – in other words the Good player may not leave the King of Rohan cowering behind the walls of the keep!

LINKING THE SCENARIOS

There are two ways to play through this book and the story of The Two Towers. The first way is to simply play each scenario in order. This is the best way to get started if you're new to The Lord of The Rings strategy battle game or wargaming in general. You and a friend can fight your way from the aftermath of Amon Hen to Osgiliath and the siege of Helm's Deep, exploring the pivotal moments from both book and film as you go along. All the scenarios follow the events in the film and the book-so even if Éomer is slain fighting the Uruk-hai who captured Merry and Pippin, you'll be able to use him at Helm's Deep.

The second way to play through this book is as a campaign, which is more challenging, but offers you the chance to see if you can do as well as the Heroes of the story without such luxuries as Heroes who come back from supposedly mortal wounds! For example, if Erkenbrand is killed at the Fords of Isen, then he won't be leading the charge at Helm's Deep… Nobody said saving the world from evil was going to be easy, did they? It's great when the outcome of each game affects what happens in future scenarios, so if you fancy playing the scenarios this way, ignore any special rules that alter a member of the Fellowship's Might, Will or Fate.

WEARY WITH MUCH TOIL?

If you want to connect your scenarios together in a campaign, you'll need to keep track of how badly injured the Heroes are, but don't worry, this isn't any more work than normal. After all, you already keep note of Might, Will, Fate and Wounds, during games. The way the scenarios are written, it's assumed that the Heroes have sufficient time to rest between battles and so restore their precious reserves of Might, Will and Fate, as well as heal any wounds that they have suffered. Realistically though, the hardships of their journeys are less likely to allow this to happen and they may find themselves locked in combat before they are fully rested.

RECOVERING RESERVES

To determine how well the Heroes have recovered after each scenario, simply nominate a surviving Hero and roll a dice for each point of characteristic that has been spent or lost. Start with Might, and then move on to Will, Fate, Courage and Wounds. On a roll of 1, 2 or 3, the Hero has not rested sufficiently and starts the next game without that characteristic point restored. On the roll of 4, 5 or 6, that point has been restored and can be used in the next game. If the Hero has any Might, they may use it to modify the dice roll as normal, though you can't attempt to recover this Might point until after the next scenario. Roll for each Hero in turn, noting any changes as you go.

For example: Legolas has had a hard time in Scenario One (Let's Hunt Some Orc) – he's lost 2 Might points, and 1 Fate point. At the end of the scenario, roll two dice to try to recover his Might points. Say you roll a 2 and a 6; that's enough to recover a single point of Might. Then if you roll a 3 when attempting to recover his Fate point, it's too bad for Legolas – he's going to have to go on without it. However, deciding that the Fate point is needed more than a point of Might, you could spend 1 Might point to change the 3 to a 4 and so recover the Fate point. Legolas would then start the next game with 1 Might, 2 Will and 2 Fate.

IT'S ONLY A FLESH WOUND... OR IS IT?

Of course, given how dangerous it is during the War of the Ring, it's quite likely that a Hero could actually be reduced to 0 wounds in the course of a scenario and 'slain'. In reality, they probably haven't been killed, but have only suffered an incapacitating blow or passed out from blood loss, or some other, not immediately fatal, occurrence. When this happens, you can use the same process described above to try and revive them – clearly the Hero's friends have carried their prone companion away from danger. In such cases you may only roll to recover Wounds, not any other profile characteristic. If you fail to recover one or more Wounds on the Hero's profile then that hero has died and their role in the tale is over.

For example, say Sam loses all of his Wounds. At the end of the scenario, you'd roll to see if he can recover either Wound. He rolls a 1 and a 3 and, tragically, Sam dies of his wounds. If Sam has a Might point remaining, now would be an excellent time to use it!

VICTORY AND DEFEAT

Regardless of the outcome of each scenario, the Heroes are assumed to have moved on to the next stage (carrying their wounded or abandoning their dead, as necessary). However, the victor of each scenario literally holds the power of life and death over the Good Heroes.

If the Good player wins the scenario he may re-roll a single dice when attempting to recover a characteristic point. If the Evil player wins the scenario, he may force the Good player to re-roll a single dice when a member of the Fellowship attempts to recover any characteristic point (awww, and it looked like Pippin was going to pull through...). Only one dice may be re-rolled – you may not re-roll one per member of the Fellowship.

THE HERO OF THE HOUR

Some members of the Fellowship have exceptional skills that affect either their recovery, or that of their comrades:

Aragorn is a knowledgeable healer, able to preserve life where others would have failed. If Aragorn is still alive at the end of a scenario, you may add 1 to a single roll when trying to recover any Hero's characteristic points.

Gimli is as stubborn as any Dwarf, and possesses powers of great endurance. Gimli will recover any characteristic point on a 3, 4, 5 or 6, rather than a 4, 5 or 6.

Frodo possesses great will, a trait that enables him to bear the Ring. Frodo will recover Will points on a roll of a 2, 3, 4, 5 or 6.

WINNING THE CAMPAIGN

The Good player wins The Two Towers campaign by playing through all the scenarios with the Ring remaining in the possession of one of his Heroes. If Frodo is slain, one of the other members of the Fellowship will take up the Ring – the Good player may choose which at the end of the scenario. However, not having the famous Baggins' fortitude, whomsoever takes on the burden must take a Courage test at the start of each of their moves. If the test is failed, remove the model from play – they have fled with the Ring (possibly muttering the word 'precious' under their breath as they go). At this point, the Good player loses the campaign and the Evil player is triumphant and darkness covers the land! Feel free to laugh evilly at this point...

GOOD HEROES

Tall and strong, Erkenbrand is Lord of the Westfold of Rohan and it is said that the valour of the legendary Helm Hammerhand lives again in him. With the death of King Théoden's son, Théodred, at the First Battle of the Fords of Isen, Erkenbrand becomes the commander of all Rohan's western defences.

Erkenbrand, Captain of Rohan (Man) Points value: 65

	F	S	D	A	W	C	M/W/F
Erkenbrand	5/4+	4	7	2	2	4	3 / 1 / 1

Wargear
Erkenbrand wears heavy armour and is equipped with a sword and shield. He also carries the Horn of the Hammerhand. At an additional cost, he may have the following:

Horse ....10 points

Special Rules
Expert Rider. See the Rohan Outrider entry opposite.

Horn of the Hammerhand. The sound of the Horn of the Hammerhand fills the men of Rohan with courage and strength. Once per game, at the beginning of any Fight phase, Erkenbrand may blow the Horn of the Hammerhand. For the duration of that fight, any Rohan models on the battlefield count as being within 3"/8cm of a banner.

Háma is the Doorward of King Théoden of Rohan and Captain of the King's Guard. Fiercely loyal to Théoden, his loyalty is unquestioned and his bravery renowned throughout the land of the Horse-lords.

Háma, Captain of Rohan (Man) Points value: 50

	F	S	D	A	W	C	M/W/F
Háma	4/4+	4	6	2	2	4	2 / 1 / 0

Wargear
Háma wears heavy armour and is equipped with a sword. At an additional cost, he may have the following:

Horse ....10 points

Special Rules
Expert Rider. See the Rohan Outrider entry opposite.

Bodyguard. Háma is sworn to protect the life of the King of Rohan. If the Good force includes Théoden, Háma will automatically pass all Courage tests he has to take so long as Théoden is alive. If Théoden is killed, Háma reverts to the normal rules for Courage.

Théodred is the only son of Théoden, King of Rohan. Strong and bold, he is a mighty and fearless warrior and a thorn in the side of Saruman and his plans. As the second Marshal of the Mark he commands a significant body of warriors and the respect of every warrior of the Rohirrim.

Théodred, Heir of Rohan (Man) Points value: 70

	F	S	D	A	W	C	M/W/F
Théodred	5/4+	4	6	2	2	5	3 / 3 / 0

Wargear:
Théodred carries a sword and wears heavy armour. At an additional cost he may have the following:

Throwing spear ....5 points
Bow ....5 points
Shield ....5 points
Horse ....10 points

Special Rules
Expert Rider. See the Rohan Outrider entry opposite.

Though all Rider of Rohan are experts in the saddle, Outriders must be exceptional even amongst their peers, scouting ahead of the main Rohan forces and laying ambushes for enemy warriors.

Rohan Outrider (Man) — Points value: 10

	F	S	D	A	W	C	M/W/F
Rohan Outrider	3/3+	3	4	1	1	3	0 / 0 / 1
Horse	0	3	4	0	1	3	

Wargear
Rohan Outriders wear armour and are equipped with a sword and a bow. At an additional cost, they may have the following:

Horse .... *5 points*

Special Rules
Expert Rider. Models that are expert riders can re-roll the dice on the Jump chart when jumping an obstacle while mounted. In addition, when mounted they benefit from the +1 Defence from their shield even while carrying a bow. If they dismount or are thrown, they must immediately discard either their bow or their shield (in which case their Defence is reduced by 1 point).

Sméagol and Gollum are two sides of the same coin, the two warring personalities of a creature obsessed with The One Ring. The kindness of Frodo Baggins gives Sméagol a chance to push the vile and murderous Gollum aside for a while, and allow his true character to rise to the fore.

Sméagol — Points value: 25

	F/S	S	D	A	W	C	M/W/F
Sméagol	4/4+	4	4	2	2	4	1 / 0 / 1

Wargear
Sméagol wears no armour and carries no weapons. His strong, strangling fingers and tricksy cunning is all he needs. Sméagol is never considered unarmed.

Special Rules
Serve the master of the precious. Sméagol has sworn to serve Frodo Baggins, the bearer of The One Ring. Sméagol may only be included in a force that also includes Frodo Baggins.

Cave Dweller. No dice is rolled when making a Jumping or Climbing test for Sméagol. Instead, the test is automatically passed as if a 6 had been rolled.

Ents are the shepherds of the trees, and once roamed in all the great forests of Middle-earth. Now their numbers are dwindling and they are a much scarcer sight, seen only in the depths of Fangorn Forest, hard on the east slopes of the Misty Mountains. Untroubled by the wider world, it is rare for Ents to interfere with affairs in the lands outside their forest.

Ent

Points value: 120

	F	S	D	A	W	C
Ent	7/4+	8	8	3	3	6

Wargear

Ents require no weaponry, using their thick, branch limbs to crush their opponents to death.

Special Rules

Break Stone. Ents are powerful creatures with iron-hard limbs that can smash apart stone just as tree roots can crumble rock. When attacking fortifications, including doors, stone walls, towers, and anything else that has Batter points, Ents count their Strength as 10 and Attacks as 6.

Terror.

Throw Stone. Ents are creatures of great strength, able to tear rocks out of the ground and hurl them across the battlefield with crushing force. To represent this, if an Ent does not move at all he can rip a suitable rock from the ground (provided he's not engaged in combat) and in the subsequent Shoot phase he can throw it. This works exactly like a crossbow with a range of 18"/42cm and a Strength of 10. If the Good player wishes, this rock can be hurled at a castle wall or other building. If this is the case, the Good player nominates a target point and rolls to hit and to wound as normal. If the shot causes sufficient damage to create a breach, the breach occurs at the point the shot was aimed at.

Woodland Creature. See main rules manual.

The Osgiliath Veterans are a dour and grim band and are the warriors that recaptured the city alongside Boromir of the White Tower. Though their armour is pitted and scarred and they carry dozens of small wounds, their fighting spirit is undiminished. Osgiliath may be ruined, a shadow of its former glory, but with their lives they defend it, proud and defiant to the end.

Osgiliath Veteran (Man)

Points value: 8

	F	S	D	A	W	C
Osgiliath Veteran	3/4+	3	5	1	1	4

Wargear

Osgiliath Veterans carry a hand weapon and are clad in dented and battle-scarred heavy armour. At an additional cost they may carry the following:

Bow .... *1 point*
Spear .... *1 point*
Shield .... *1 point*

Special Rules:

Loyal to the Captains. The Osgiliath Veterans have fought alongside Boromir and Faramir for months, if not years, and each one of them is loyal unto death. So long as an Osgiliath Veteran is within 6"/14cm of either Boromir or Faramir (or both) he receives a bonus of +1 to its Fight value.

EVIL HEROES

Vraskû, Uruk-hai Scout Captain (Uruk-hai) — Points value: 60

Vraskû commands the legions of the White Hand Scout Uruk-hai. A cunning and resourceful leader, Vraskû is utterly ruthless and heedless of the lives of his followers, so long as the will of Isengard is enacted.

	F	S	D	A	W	C	M/W/F
Vraskû	5/3+	5	5	2	2	4	3 / 1 / 1

Wargear
Vraskû is armed with a crossbow, a sword and wears armour.

Special Rules
Expert Shot. Vraskû is allowed to shoot his specially modified crossbow twice in the Shoot phase instead of just once.

Uglúk (Uruk-hai) — Points value: 60

With Lurtz slain by Aragorn at Amon Hen, and the hunters still hot on their heels, it is Uglúk that rises to the fore amongst the Orcs carrying Merry and Pippin back to Saruman. A savage character, Uglúk keeps his followers in check with a combination of crude cunning and open brutality.

	F	S	D	A	W	C	M/W/F
Uglúk	5/4+	5	5	2	2	4	3 / 1 / 1

Wargear
Uglúk carries a sword and wears heavy armour.

Special Rules:
Head Taker. Uglúk is unshakably loyal to Saruman and thinks nothing of setting about his followers to make an example of them and keep order in the ranks. Instead of rolling the dice to make a Courage test when the Evil force is Broken, Uglúk can remove any Evil model in base contact from play. If he does this Uglúk is considered to have passed his Courage test and his Stand Fast! has a range of 12"/28cm

Dunlending Chieftain (Man) — Points value: 50

Only the most violent and savage of warriors can rise to prominence in Dunlending society, and only those who excel in personal combat can hope to last any length of time. Respect is earned by feats of martial prowess, and any that claim the title of chieftain must protect their position from all who covet it.

	F	S	D	A	W	C	M/W/F
Dunlending Chieftain	4/4+	4	5	2	2	4	2 / 3 / 1

Wargear
A Dunlending Chieftain carries a hand weapon and wears battered and worn armour. At an additional cost he may carry the following:

Bow . . . . *5 points*
Shield . . . . *5 points*
Two-handed axe . . . . *5 points*

EVIL WARRIORS

Following the example of his master, Sauron, the Wizard Saruman has bred his Trolls bigger and stronger than their subterranean cousins. Resistant to sunlight and armoured in the fashion of the Uruk-hai, Isengard Trolls are terrifying opponents and can easily slay all but the most powerful opponents.

Isengard Troll — Points value: 105

	F	S	D	A	W	C
Isengard Troll	6/5+	6	8	3	3	4

Wargear
An Isengard Troll wears heavy plates of armour, carries a shield and a hand weapon. At an additional cost, an Isengard Troll may have the following:

Spear . . . . 1 point

Special Rules.
Terror.

Throw Stones. If a Troll does not move at all, he can declare he's 'stooping for a stone', and in the subsequent Shoot phase he can throw it, provided that he is not engaged in combat. This works exactly like a crossbow with a range of 12"/28cm and a Strength of 8.

The long-dead warriors of forgotten battlefields, these watery revenants of Orcs, Men and Elves cast their ghostly light over marshes and sites of ancient darkness. Their very presence foretells death and their pellucid glow lures the unwitting to their doom with beguiling lights and unearthly magic.

Spectre (Spirit) — Points value: 15

	F	S	D	A	W	C
Spectre	2/-	3	5	1	1	6

Wargear
Spectres wear ancient heavy armour and are armed with swords of great antiquity.

Special Rules
Terror.

A Fell light is in them. The fey lights and beguiling glow of the Spectres can lull the senses of enemies and lure them to their doom. At any point in the Move phase, choose a single enemy model within 12"/28cm of the Spectre to be targeted by the lure of its fell light. The targeted model must pass a Courage test or it will make a full move under the control of the Evil player, even if it has already moved – though models may not be moved out of combat. This move cannot be used to enter another model's control zone, or perform an action than would cause harm to the target (such as jumping down a cliff etc), though it can be used to move them into areas of marsh or bog. The model cannot be forced to lie down, climb, jump, mount, dismount or other complex movements. Affected models may not move further that turn.

Bred from the Orcs of Minas Morgul, these twisted creatures came into being by the will and evil malice of the Witch-king to keep safe his domain from intruders. Armoured and cloaked in the image of their master, Morgul Stalkers are swift moving, silent killers.

Morgul Stalker (Orc) — Points value: 15

	F	S	D	A	W	C
Morgul Stalker	3/-	4	4	2	1	3

Wargear

Morgul Stalkers are sometimes armed with swords, though their slashing claws and razor sharp fangs make equally fearsome weapons.

Special Rules.

Shadow Haunters. Morgul Stalkers move through the darkness like shadows unbound, slipping unseen through the night to slay their foes before their victims even know they are there. Morgul Stalkers always count as though they are equipped with Elven cloaks.

The Dunlendings bear unequalled animosity to the Men of Rohan. They call them the forgoil, the strawheads, and have hated them for five hundred years. In battle they are ferocious, fighting with round shields and sharp axes. Though they lack the finesse of other, better-trained soldiers, the warriors of Dunland are a formidable enemy to face.

Dunlending Warrior (Man) — Points value: 6

	F	S	D	A	W	C
Dunlending Warrior	3/4+	3	4	1	1	3

Wargear

Dunlending warriors carry a hand weapon and are clad in battered and worn armour. At an additional cost they may carry the following:

Bow ....1 point
Two-handed axe ....1 point
Shield ....1 point
Banner ....25 points

Uruk-hai are already brutal fighters, but there are those driven to madness by torture from their own kind in order to breed an unthinking hostility to all living things. Kept chained in the deepest dungeons of Isengard, these bestial Uruk-hai lust for carnage and live only for the shedding of blood.

Feral Uruk-hai — Points value: 12

	F	S	D	A	W	C
Feral Uruk-hai	4/-	4	5	2	1	5

Wargear

Feral Uruk-hai wear armour and carry two swords.

SUMMARY

	F	S	D	A	W	C	M/W/F	Special Rules
Erkenbrand	5/4+	4	7	2	2	4	3 / 1 / 1	Expert Rider; Horn of the Hammerhand
Háma	4/4+	4	6	2	2	4	2 / 1 / 0	Expert Rider; Bodyguard
Théodred	5/4+	4	6	2	2	5	3 / 3 / 0	Expert Rider
Rohan Outriders	3/3+	3	4	1	1	3	0 / 0 / 1	Expert Rider
Sméagol	4/4+	4	4	2	2	4	1 / 0 / 1	Serve the Master of the Precious; Cave Dweller
Ents	7/4+	8	8	3	3	6		Break Stone; Throw Stone; Terror
Osgiliath Veterans	3/4+	3	5	1	1	4		Loyal to the Captains
Vraskû	5/3+	5	5	2	2	4	3 / 1 / 1	Expert Shot
Uglúk	5/4+	5	5	2	2	4	3 / 1 / 1	Head Taker
Dunlending Chieftain	4/4+	4	5	2	2	4	2 / 3 / 1	
Spectres	2/-	3	5	1	1	6		Terror; A Fell light is in them
Isengard Troll	6/5+	6	8	3	3	4		Terror; Throw Stones
Morgul Stalkers	3/-	4	4	2	1	3		Shadow Stalkers
Dunlending Warrior	3/4+	3	4	1	1	3		
Feral Uruk-hai	4/-	4	5	2	1	5		
Horse	0	3	4	0	1	3